TERESA ST. FRANCES
COMMUNICATES

WHAT HAPPENS
THE DAY AFTER?
MESSAGES FROM ADOLESCENT SUICIDES

AETHREAL
PRODUCTIONS, LLC

What Happens the Day After?
Messages from Adolescent Suicides

by Teresa St. Frances

ISBN: 978-0-9776282-0-3 (Paperback)

Published by:

AETHREAL
PRODUCTIONS, LLC

New Jersey

Cover and Interior design by
Scotty Roberts
www.scottalanroberts.com

WHAT HAPPENS
THE DAY AFTER?
MESSAGES FROM ADOLESCENT SUICIDES

DEDICATION

To my Aunt Meme and Uncle Joe who have shown me how to love, and demonstrated what love truly is. I am forever your daughter, for without your love I would not be the person I am today.

There is family by choice and family by birth. To Kathy and Brad Gibbons my family by choice, you will never know how deeply you have touched me, for when I had no one you both gave me a home within your hearts. You have opened up your home to my kids when I was unable to care for them, allowing me time to heal. And that was one of the greatest gifts you have given me. For all the things that you have done, you have helped make this book a reality.

My "TAG TEAM," for without your loving support and constant guidance I would not have been able to sustain my life.

Michelle, for being my assistant, and for guiding those in the afterlife to my door to tell their stories. All of you will be forever in my prayers and thoughts.

ACKNOWLEDGMENTS

*f*amily by choice has been my saving grace.

To my sisters by choice:

Cheryl C., I could not have completed this book without your help, support and love. During the times I was unsure about this book, you were my rock and cheerleader. I will always be grateful for our connection.

Kelly G., Your invaluable friendship, insight and support has always been a blessing. If it was not for your technology and marketing knowledge, I know I would not be where I am today.

Yolanda D. If it was not for your wisdom and knowledge I would be truly alone on this planet. Thank you for always being there when I had health issues. Your understanding always put my mind at ease.

Ariana D., you became my muse, for that clandestine lunch forged the outline for this book. Thank You.

The beautiful Ladies who helped me when I did not who to turn to for help at the time of my spiritual crisis, I will forever be grateful to you for your loving help and support.

Laura W., You are forever in my thoughts and prayers.

Aggie A, for always taking my calls and giving me the support and business advice that kept me on solid ground.

Frank C., no matter how busy you were, you always had time for me and have helped me in ways that I can never repay.

To my clients who have allowed me to share your readings in the book I am deeply grateful.

To my all my clients who have allowed me to help them. I am honored that you have supported me and encouraged me to continue even when I thought I could not.

To the many people along the way who were helpful with the book including Alice P. and Eda A. Thank You for all the time and effort.

Teresa
New Jersey
May, 2016

TABLE
OF CONTENTS

FOREWORD
BY JENNY McCARTHY

*L*ife is wonderful.

Despite all its ups and downs, its hairpin curves and its roller-coaster-ish peaks and valleys, Life is an awesome experience. I love my Life and I wouldn't trade it for anyone or anything. And I certainly could never see myself leaving this Life - or taking my Life - at the far end of sadness, despair or hopelessness. That just isn't who I am, and it isn't what I want.

But that is not true for everyone. And I sometimes wonder what it is that brings someone to the point where they would desire to end their own Life. Why do people become so overwhelmed by the things they experience as obstacles, hardships and pain, that they would come to the conclusion that ending their Life is better than living it?

The saddest end to the wonder of Life is when someone is so heartbroken, grieving or despondent, that committing suicide is, for them, at that moment, the only way to stop their pain. Even sadder yet, is when a young person, engulfed in whatever malaise of suffering they are experiencing, sees their Life as having no more meaning, and they snuff out their brilliant, beautiful light with their own hands.

Ending a Life by suicide leaves an even deeper, sadder, gaping hole, when it is committed by the hands of a teenager who will never have the chance to live their Life to its fullest. They've cut themselves off from their Life, and they have ended the plan designed for them, before they've ever begun to really live it. And in the wake are left moms and dads, siblings and grandparents, family and friends who struggle to find the answers that will never truly be realized. All they have left is the emptiness that is filled only with the echoing of their sobs and unanswered questions.

I am reminded of the words of Thoreau, as paraphrased in the movie, *Dead Poets Society*, that poignantly dealt with teen suicide, *"I went to the woods because I wanted to live deliberately. I wanted to live deep and suck out all the marrow of Life. To put to rout all that was not Life; and not, when I had come to die, discover that I had not lived."*

"Not lived," is Life as defined by teen suicide. And it all seems so hopeless and sad.

But there is a Life beyond this Life. I have always been a spiritual person, and I have always held the belief that there is something more beyond the veil of this Life. Some of us define that with religion, some of us with consciousness studies, but none of us really knows beyond a shadow of a doubt that there is an afterLife. And even when we do believe it exists, we hold to so many different interpretations and beliefs, that we are left unsure of anything beyond a distant hope or that warm fuzzy feeling.

But what do you do when someone speaks with a voice that pierces the veil? What amazing realization comes rushing in when a kid who's taken their own Life finds a way to express why they did what they did, and what they are experiencing on that other plane. Many times they try to tell us through small signs and things that we can sometimes miss when we aren't tuned in to looking and listening for what they have to say. We are so involved with our daily lives that we forget to look! And we can miss the beautiful messages sent our way.

Teresa has written a wonderful book, completely filled with pathos and sadness, yet delivering an unswerving message that speaks with the voice of those teenage kids who took their own lives. They have found a voice in Teresa, who I would call an almost unwitting medium for these kids to once again speak out loud to the living. Page after page I found myself overwhelmed and sometimes in tears as I read the words of these kids speaking from the other side.

If you are skeptical of the spiritual, you may find this book difficult to swallow. But even more, you will live a Life that is void of knowing anything beyond the tangible. The universe is a pretty big place, and it is filled with Life and wonder. Here in these pages, you will find the tragedy of Life ended too soon, but the hope of knowing that Life goes on and can speak to us if we are open enough to listen.

Jenny McCarthy
Los Angeles, CA
May, 2016

INTRODUCTION
WHY I HAVE WRITTEN THIS BOOK

*M*y entire life I've seen the world differently.

It all began when I was about four years old, and I could see colors around people. I remember sitting outside and looking ahead towards the mountains, just above the treetops, looking at the vibrancy that emanated from the trees. I didn't think it was anything unusual. I thought that everybody saw what I saw: the glow that surrounds people, animals and trees.

My initial spiritual experience occurred at a family Fourth of July picnic. My parents were showing old family movies on their 8 mm reel projector of people who had already crossed over into the light. I recall these people identifying themselves to me and explaining what had happened to them.

I revealed this information to my mother. My mother's response was, "We are Catholic, and we go to church every week. You're never to speak a word about this to anyone." Mother's rules were law; therefore, I never spoke about it again.

Throughout my childhood, **SPIRITS surrounded me.** Relatives would express their concern as they witnessed me talking to myself. It was beyond their comprehension. One Friday evening, a storm was raging and I was frightened! At the foot of my bed, I saw a floating, lavender **ANGEL**.

This magnificent vision smiled at me, and my fear immediately vanished. The angel spoke to me via my thoughts. Her message was for me to never be afraid because she was my **GUARDIAN ANGEL.** She would be there to guide me always.

Through the years, I have had many interactions with my **GUARDIAN ANGEL.** Besides being my guide, protector, and my **divine LIGHT, she is my true friend.**

Unfortunately, over the course of my life, I have been unable to escape some unforeseen, quite serious, life threatening health issues. However, none of these define me. I am a firm believer that things happen for a reason/reasons and sometimes we cannot comprehend why. I believe that it was my destiny to experience, fight, and win my battles to serve an as instrument to help others win their battles, as well.

During my youth, there were no psychic role models. I did not know what I was experiencing was unusual. I watched television and saw many of the things happening in my life being acted out on the shows. I thought if it was on television, then it was normal, and everybody experienced the same phenomena as I did. Growing up I did not aspire to be a gifted spiritual messenger. I was told that being able to know things, without having any physical proof before they happen and speaking with the deceased was taboo. Even in today's society being a psychic medium is a controversial issue. However, I can confidently say that within the last 20 years most of society has changed their views of psychic mediums. For me, my divine experiences and lessons I was learning as an adolescent were extremely difficult to understand because there was no teacher or manual. I was ignorant. At times, not being able to handle it all, I felt as though I was cursed. Only when I was in my late 20's did I start to understand what it meant to be a gifted spiritual messenger. My faith and connection with my **"TAG TEAM"** have enabled me to accept and embrace full ownership of who I am.

I grew up in a traditional, dysfunctional Italian Catholic household where what went on behind closed doors was to be kept behind closed doors. My family life was a game of secrets and lies. I am the oldest of three girls, and as I grew up, I became the outcast of the family because I was able to see **SPIRITS** and have conversations with them. Growing up, I kept to myself and didn't have any friends. In school I was always bullied because of my weight; often being the victim of demeaning remarks and harassing jokes. I never felt as though I belonged anywhere. I was the outcast. I didn't belong in my family, in school or in society.

During these years, I found great refuge in the woods. I reveled in many delightful hours connecting with Mother Nature. This unique experience made me cognizant of my love, respect and understanding of all creatures, which has helped build the foundation of who I am today.

The first realization that I was not like everyone else occurred during my first year in agricultural college while studying to be large animal veterinarian. My first semester classes were farm based, and on a hot humid day in late August I was walking down the path approaching the swine pen. All the pigs were on the opposite side of the pen wallowing in mud. I opened the pen door, and I saw other students standing up on the hill looking down towards the pigs. I walked towards them with my back to the pigs and I felt the earth shake! I turned around and all the pigs were running towards me! They surrounded me and lifted me off my feet!

I was scared because I had no experience with pigs I was never lifted off my feet before by **ANYONE,** let alone animals! I looked at the other students. They all stood there in amazement! I did not know what else to do but ask for help. Not one student came to my aid. The pigs kept me surrounded, but I felt that they didn't want to hurt me. I relaxed, and I could hear them in my thoughts telling me about them. I could feel their love and happiness

I looked up at my classmates. They were all looking at me as though I was someone not of this world. I was questioning why these pigs were surrounding me and not gravitating towards anyone else?

The pigs followed me throughout the entire class. My teacher and all my fellow classmates gave me glaring looks because the pigs were so loud, and they drowned out the lecture. This made me very uncomfortable. I was feeling as though I was the outsider because this was not happening to anyone else. By the end of class, my classmates wanted nothing to do with me. Once again, I was the outcast.

Our next class was at the horse barn. As soon as I entered the barn, all the horses stuck their heads out of their stalls and started making a fuss, kicking their doors and talking. They wanted me to stop and talk with them! I was attentive to some, but I needed to catch up with the rest of the class. The teacher and my classmates were in the horse paddock continuing to eye me up and down giving me strange looks. The horses were noisy throughout the whole class. This occurred almost every time I went to the barns.

In retrospect, this was my training ground for the work I do today communicating with living, as well as deceased animals.

I always knew I was different, but I tried to conform and adjust into the mainstream of life. Most people have a hard time adjusting to college. For me it was even more difficult. I had many challenging experiences. As a result, I suffered from situational depression.

There were many times when I contemplated what life would be like if I were not alive. I even tried committing suicide by driving a car into a telephone pole.

I woke up in the hospital seeing my **GUARDIAN ANGEL** and many other **ANGELS** around my bed talking about me. They did not realize I was awake. When they did realize that I was awake they removed themselves. My **GUARDIAN ANGEL** stayed and spoke to me in my thoughts telling me that trying to take my own life was not the answer to my problems. She told me that they pulled me out of the car, and that is why I have no major damage to my body.

They saved me.

I wound up with a scraped knee and a cut on my head. The car was totaled. The doctors were amazed that although I had crushed the steering wheel into a pretzel shape, and had gone through the windshield, I only had minor injuries.

My **GUARDIAN ANGEL** told me that my purpose on Earth is to help people and that I was to remain here to fulfill my **LIFE CONTRACT.** I was in and out of conscientiousness at the time, and I told her she needed to go; I was skeptical. I had nothing to offer anyone. I recovered from the accident without any medical issues.

There was an investigation that determined the road was slick causing me to lose control of the car. I went back to college still feeling detached from life and struggled with my thoughts and feelings.

During the course of my life, I had a few more failed attempts at suicide. Each time my **GUARDIAN ANGEL** would appear, as well as my **"TAG TEAM,"** and instructed me that I was to stay alive to complete my calling written in my **LIFE CONTRACT.**

Our **LIFE CONTRACT** is an outline of our life written by us with **THE CREATOR** and our **"TAG TEAM"** participating from the **HEAVENS.** This agreement is comingled to include everyone and everything in our lives. This contract includes not only the outline it also contains clauses that could be invoked to keep us on the agreed upon path. We signed on the dotted line and accepted the terms of the contract before we were born.

We all have a spiritual family that I refer to as my **"TAG TEAM,"** which represents loving teachers and angels. They orchestrate from behind the scenes to help support, guide and protect us throughout life. They help ensure that we are following our destiny.

After I graduated from college, I moved into my first apartment. I didn't know it was haunted. The **SPIRIT** which resided in my apartment, fondly known as Al, became my spiritual awakening. Al would move things and re-arrange my house during the night. I would wake and things would be moved or the refrigerator door would be open. He was trying to scare me out of my apartment and was doing a good job!

He said I was the only tenant that he could not get to move and that he used my gifts to frighten me.

During this time I developed my ability to feel **SPIRIT** and speak to them as though I was speaking to the living. This new communication platform elevated me to a higher level, which took me time to understand. As for AL I did not realize that a **SPIRIT** could attach itself to an apartment. This was my introduction to **SPIRITS** who have crossed over but not into the **LIGHT of HEAVEN.** I realized that I was ill equipped to deal with Al.

I sought help and found a group of woman who were quietly practicing their psychic medium abilities. They came to my home and we did a circle séance.

Al came through, wanting his apartment back!

He did not realize that he was dead. He was a lost soul.

After a few days of trying to get Al to understand his circumstances, things got worse, not better. These women realized that they needed more help. The next day we all sat in another séance and these beautiful women invoked the **ANGELIC REALM** and asked for the **ANGELIC HIERARCHY** to come and assist. For the first time in my life, I saw **ARCHANGEL MICHAEL.**

ARCHANGEL MICHAEL and his legion of **ANGELS** opened up the **HEAVENS** and moved Al into **HEAVEN.**   It was then that I realized **HEAVEN** is the most beautiful, loving place to live. **ARCHANGEL MICHAEL** turned around to face me and said that he would be back for me. In my head I was thinking "Hurray. I get to go home."

After several weeks of quiet peaceful living in my apartment, things changed. One night I was awakened by **ARCHANGEL MICHAEL, MY GUARDIAN ANGEL** and my **"TAG TEAM."** They were all in my bedroom, and all of them were tugging on my sheets!

I asked them what they wanted and they answered that it was now time for me to awaken and fulfill my **LIFE CONTRACT.** I told them I wanted to go back to bed since I had to go to work the next day and to leave me alone.

I was working in New York City at the time, and the commute was grueling. They did leave me alone that night. However, they came back earlier each night afterward, being persistent until I agreed to talk with them.

I was to work with them every night, being instructed on how to use my gifts to open up the innate wisdom and knowledge that was in my soul. I did this through meditating and practicing breath work to open my **SPIRITUAL** conduits to the HEAVENS.

The women who helped me with AL often held a private development circle. They invited me to join them so they could instruct me how to balance my earthly and spiritual worlds. This was my training ground for the work I do today.

I did not grow up wanting to be a gifted spiritual messenger. I wanted to be a vet. However, due to many obstacles out of my control, I decided to go into sales and marketing, and ultimately became a Vice-President of a telecommunications firm in New Jersey.

During the same period I was opening up and growing spiritually.

SPIRIT kept telling me that I needed to leave my professional life and step into the **MASTER PLAN.**

I asked them what they meant, and I was told that each one of us has a unique **LIFE CONTRACT** that we need to fulfill. The contract is a binding agreement between the **CREATOR** and us and that there are things that we agreed upon. My life contract was designed to help others, thereby fulfilling a greater plan or **MASTER PLAN.**

They explained that all of humanity is tied together for the purpose of raising the spiritual energy on this planet. I was expected to help people reach their full potential by doing spiritual readings to help them heal. I told them I did not want to do spiritual readings. I had a great job, and I was financially secure.

Knowing that I might be obstinate, they told me that a clause existed and would be evoked if I did not listen to them. The clause stated that something would happen to change my direction if I did not do it for myself.

Every night for a year we would have this conversation. I would thank them for teaching me my lessons and tell them that I loved them, but that I was not giving up my position as Vice President. One All Hallows Eve, coming home from a business trip, I had a severe car accident.

The limo was hit by another car and wrapped around a telephone pole. This threw me to the front seat, although I was a passenger in the back of the limo.

The other driver vanished, and they never found the other car. I walked out of the limo alive, but sustained many internal injuries from which it took me eighteen months to recover.

This accident, as they had told me, was in my contract as a clause to be invoked if I did not listen.

That accident was the turning point in my life. It put me on my path to the professional work I do today. It taught me how to heal people. It gave me the opportunity to share my spiritual knowledge and wisdom through readings, events, lectures, classes and workshops.

I am a gifted spiritual messenger connecting the two worlds to bring forth loving messages from the afterlife.

In recent years, more than ever before, I find myself delivering more messages from adolescent suicides to friends and family members.

Privately, at night, I have visitors who are lost and through my help I bring them into the **LIGHT of HEAVEN.**

I have also been speaking with many young adolescent visitors who committed suicide and reside in HEAVEN. Through this process they wanted to share their stories and tell those alive that there is a bigger picture. It is just not about high school or college; it is about **LIVING A FULL INTERCONNECTED, LONG LIFE.**

The pain I feel when I talk with them has left a lifetime impression and changed my life forever.

I decided to write this book to open a dialogue and create awareness that change is needed at home, in school, in society, in religion, in the medical community and throughout the world.

My hope is that by reading the book a chain reaction of new ideas and actions will begin that alter the lives of many young adolescents.

My prayer is for all of you who are grieving for a friend or family member, maybe a daughter or son, who has taken his or her life, to find comfort in reading this book.

If this book changes the mind of one person who is contemplating suicide, then I have done my job by changing a piece of the world.

My goal in writing this book is to change lives by fostering the awareness in all individuals of how very precious and short-termed our lives really are, to embrace our blessings, and to live life to its fullest!

CHAPTER ONE
MICHELLE'S ANGEL COMES FOR A READING

Hello...

Hello…

Hello…

Can you hear me...?

Yes, I can even see you.

What is your name?

My name is Michelle and that is my mom sitting in front of you.

Michelle: Hi Mom, I am here, and I am sorry.

Teresa: (as I hold her mother Angela's hands)
I have your daughter with me, and she's standing right next to you putting her hand on your shoulder.

Angela weeps.

Michelle stands in front of me in full body, healthy, and I proceed to give Angela a description of what I perceive. Michelle is over five-foot, five-inches tall with long brown hair, hazel eyes. She's wearing jeans, flip-flops and many bracelets on both wrists, and she is smiling. She looks to be around 20 years old.

Angela: Michelle was 19 when she passed, and how do you know what my daughter looks like? I didn't show you a picture.

Teresa: I can see your daughter as clearly as you are sitting in front of me. **SPIRITS** take the form of what they want me to see so that I can tell you how they are, and Michelle chose to take the form of what she looked like in high school. Since she has been in **SPIRIT**, Michelle has learned to re-create her physical form, and she is so happy about it.

Angela: Why high school and not college? Or how she looked when she passed?

Teresa to Michelle: Why high school?

Michelle: That was when I was the happiest. I loved life back then. Things were going well, and I was always doing well.

Before Angela could ask me any more questions, Michelle tells me that she has something very important to say to her mom.

Michelle: I do not look like what you constantly think of me in the casket, Mom. Please stop going back to me in the casket. That is not how I want to be remembered! I want you to remember me laughing and having fun. I see you watching the videos of me playing softball or us down at the shore house.

I WANT YOU TO REMEMBER ME WHEN I WAS HAPPY!! YOU ALWAYS LOVED MY LAUGH! THAT IS HOW I WANT YOU TO REMEMBER ME!!

At this point in the reading Angela was so taken aback with this information that she could not fully comprehend what Michelle was telling her. That is why I think she asked me, "Is she really here?"

I asked Michelle to tell me something only her mom would know. Michelle showed me a strawberry shaped mark on her hip.

Teresa: Is that what you want me to tell your mom?

Michelle shows me a baby.

Teresa: Michelle is showing me a strawberry mark on her hip and a baby, so this is a birthmark, not a tattoo.

Angela breaks down and cries uncontrollably. She then takes a deep breath and asks me,

"How do you know that?"

Teresa: Michelle is here with you, always.

Michelle proceeds to talk about her love of jewelry, especially bracelets. She then proceeds to show me one bracelet that has special charms. She shows me many charms on the bracelet, and she makes it a point to show me the baseball, volleyball, dog, flip-flops and the **ANGEL** charm.

Teresa to Angela: Michelle has shown me charms from her bracelet, and there is a special charm that looks like an Angel Charm. And she then gives me, what I call, my 'sign of love.' She also tells me that it has a special meaning and to make it a point to tell "her mom."

I tell Angela that the special charm that I perceive to be an **ANGEL** is extremely important because by showing me that charm, Michelle has given me my sign of **LOVE**. I also feel that I need to say to you, **"I LOVE YOU."**

Before I could get all the words out of my mouth, Angela composes herself and starts both laughing and crying at the same time.

Angela to Teresa: I bought my daughter this charm bracelet, and on special occasions I would give her a charm. Just before she left for college, I gave Michelle this **ANGEL** charm because I wanted to let her know that she was my special **ANGEL**. Since my name was Angela, I wanted her to know that she could always rely on me as her **ANGEL**.

I was very touched by this, and I got a little emotional as well. We clutched each other's hands and smiled.

Michelle's **SPIRIT** is still very strong, and she wants to continue talking with her mom. She then points to her mother's wrist and tells me that underneath her mother's sweater is the same exact charm bracelet.

Teresa: Michelle is showing me Angela wearing the same, exact charm bracelet, with one exception - Angela added the initial "M" for Michelle. Michelle also tells me that you got the bracelet in memory of her and that she was laid to rest with her own bracelet. Angela pulls up her sweater and shows me the bracelet with many charms on it. She isolates the **ANGEL** charm and turns it over. Inscribed are the words **"I LOVE YOU."**

Teresa: Do you now doubt that your daughter is with you?

Angela is still trying to compose herself. She smiles.

Angela: I really was not sure before coming into the reading, but now I know for sure that Michelle is here. How will I know that she is

14

with me when I leave? I talk to her all the time but I feel like I do not get any answers. I do not feel her at all.

She then breaks down again and weeps.

Teresa to Michelle: Have you left any signs for your mom or anybody else in the family since you passed?

Michelle: I have been trying to let her know I am there by leaving her pennies. The other day she was putting her socks on and getting ready for work,she felt something odd, and when she removed her sock there was a penny stuck to the bottom of her foot.

Teresa repeats to Angela what Michelle just told her.

Angela: Yes, yes, but it was about a week ago not a few days ago.

Teresa: SPIRITS do not always understand linear time as we do. There is no time on the other side – at least not in the same way we perceive it -and their concept of "the other day" can be as long as weeks for us.

Angela nodded and continued to eagerly listen. I explained to her that loved ones on the other side send us signs to let us know that they are here with us and that their love continues.

Michelle: I left signs for Dad, too. I have been making him smell leather, and I have played with the radio stations while he was driving, which I always did when we were in the car together.

She tells me that was one of her fondest memories, when her dad would oil her softball gloves, and he would make sure he kept them in good shape for her.

Teresa repeats to Angela what Michelle just told her.

Teresa: Can you relate to this information?

Angela: I vaguely remember John (her husband) mentioning that he had been smelling leather while he was driving his car, and he was constantly complaining about the radio stations changing.

Teresa: Tell John that those were signs from Michelle and that she is with him.

Angela: Ok. I was going to tell him that I came here for a reading and that I want him to listen to our recorded session.

Teresa: Michelle wants to talk to me about her life - can I continue?

I barely get the words out of my mouth, and Michelle is off talking about her life. She talks very fast and is animated in the way she carries herself.

Teresa: Your daughter is a type 'A' personality who had a lot of energy, always trying to help people and had a big heart. She was involved in many things. She tells me that she was captain of the softball team, played volleyball and loved to help the underdog. In school she had a lot of friends and was the girl everybody looked up to and asked for advice. She was involved in the student government and in many after school activities. She was a perfectionist. She also told me that she had a high standard for herself and she liked keeping herself in shape by running. She always had a smile on her face and did excellent in school. She tells me that she was very smart and was a straight 'A' student, something in which she prided herself. She also said that the only subject that she had to work hard in to get an A was Math. She tells me she graduated high school with honors and that was the proudest moment of her life. She also talked about her love of the shore and how, during the summer, the family spent as much time as they could at the shore house. That is why she showed me the flip-flop charm. She said that she loved wearing flip-flops instead of shoes.

Teresa: She said if she could, she would wear flip-flops all year around.

She also talks about a special bond with her father and that she felt she was "Daddy's little girl." He would bring her to all her sporting events, and he was her biggest cheerleader. She tells me that she sees him and that he does not talk much. She says that she loved being the big sister to Maria and Monica. She shows me that she was closer to Maria then Monica.

Teresa: Why?

Michelle: Because Maria and I were only 15 months apart, and Monica was 7 years younger. I did not spend a lot of time with Monica, and I now regret not doing so.

I convey all this information to Angela and she confirms that the information is accurate and highly emotional, yet confusing for her.

This confuses me a bit because so far, the information has been correct and the reading is going well.

Teresa to Angela: Why are you confused?

Angela's tone and demeanor quickly change.

Angela: Does Michelle know how she died??!! Why is she not talking about her death!!

Teresa to Michelle: How did you die?

There is a long pause in our conversation.

Michelle hesitantly says: "I do not want to discuss that."

Teresa: Why not? You have been so talkative with everything else why not tell us how you got to **HEAVEN?**

Michelle: I do not want to deal with that.

Teresa to Angela: Michelle's response is she refuses to discuss her passing.

Angela (very angry): But that is why I am here! I need to understand my daughter's death!

Teresa: I cannot force Michelle to talk about what she is unwilling to discuss. In heaven, there is free will, just like here on Earth. Michelle seems to only want to talk about happy times, not bad things. She does not want to talk about her passing, and she is very upset by this question.

Angela is now getting very angry with me because I cannot give her the information she wants so desperately.

I now make the decision to switch gears. I ask Michelle to step aside and ask her **GUARDIAN ANGEL** to comfort her, as she is very upset about this question. I call on my **"TAG TEAM"** to connect with me to gather the information that Michelle refuses to provide. I wait patiently.

Teresa to Angela: I have asked the **ANGELS** to intercede and help give me the information that you have asked for, and I am waiting for an answer. I can only give you the information that I am given.

My **"TAG TEAM"** steps forward and with loving hands they hand me what I refer to as the "remote". I take the remote and click on play. I watch on a big spiritual screen Michelle during the last moments of her life. She is highly agitated and is on top of a building pacing. She looks up, notices the deep, blue sky overhead and the sun brightly shining. As I continue to watch something comes over her, and she relaxes. She seems at peace. She goes to the far end of the building, takes a deep breath, runs to the other side and jumps.

I look over to Michelle, even though the **ANGELS** are comforting her, she is clearly upset over me seeing what she had done.

Michelle: Do not tell Mom!

Teresa: She already knows, and your mom loves you no matter what you did.

Michelle: I know that, but I did not want to disappoint them.

Teresa: (I ask her lovingly) Can I please tell your mom? It will give

18

her peace and help her heal.

Michelle embraced by her GUARDIAN ANGEL, tearfully replies, "Yes."

Teresa to Angela: My "TAG TEAM" has helped me receive the information you need and Michelle is being held in the loving arms of her **GUARDIAN ANGEL.**

We proceed to discuss Michelle's passing.

It is never easy for me to discuss a suicide. Every suicide is different and has so many emotional elements. I compose myself, take a deep breath and attempt to formulate a gentle way to talk about her daughter's decision.

Teresa: I am sorry for your loss, and I know this is hard to live with, but know that your daughter is in the **LIGHT OF HEAVEN.**

Teresa: My team has shown me that Michelle took her life by jumping off a building and that she now resides with her **GUARDIAN ANGEL.** I was shown that she was having a hard time with many things in her life at the time.

Angela bursts out crying: Why did she kill herself? She had so much to live for! Why did she not call me? Why did she not call her father? Why did she not ask for help? Why? Why? Why?

I paused for a while waiting for Angela to compose herself, which, in turn, gave me time to talk with Michelle.

Michelle, who was watching her mother's outburst, responds in a loud voice, **"I LOVE YOU, MOM!"** and then steps back out of my view.

Her **GUARDIAN ANGEL** explains to me that since Michelle has had time in **HEAVEN** to review her actions, she has been remorseful and ashamed that she hurt them (her mother and the rest of the family) and that was not her intention. I thanked her **GUARDIAN**

19

ANGEL for helping, and I asked if there was there anything I could do to help Michelle and her mom. Michelle's **GUARDIAN ANGEL** asked me to let Michelle have more time to adjust. I ask how long has Michelle been in the **HEAVENS.** The **GUARDIAN ANGEL** gave me the number '3.' And with that, the **ANGEL** also moved outside of my view. The connection closes and I take a deep breath.

As I always do, I thanked everyone for assisting in today's conversation and that only LOVE and LIGHT remain.

Teresa: Angela, before Michelle left, she said in a loud voice,"I **LOVE YOU, MOM!"**

Angela by this time is quite shaken and emotionally overwhelmed. She starts to sob deeply and uncontrollably. I waited for a while and proceeded to talk to her about the "number 3" in reference to her daughter's passing.

Teresa: The number '3' was referenced, and I am not sure what that means. There is no time on the other side, there are no clocks, so was it three months, three years or did she pass on the third day?

Angela (emotionally exhausted): It's been three months since my **ANGEL** took her life.

I now understood why the reading went the way it did. Both Michelle and Angela had not had sufficient time to process the events.

Michelle has not had enough time to adjust to the other side, and her mother is still grieving and very angry.

Teresa: My rule of thumb is a minimum of six months after a person passes before family or friends try to contact their dearly departed.

Each **SPIRIT** is different in how long it takes to adjust to the other side. I have experienced **SPIRITS** who come back and speak with me within a week after their passing. I have also spoken with **SPIRITS** who passed and have been there for over a hundred years, and they are still in the Healing Hospital. There are no rules or time frame on the other side or for how a **SPIRIT** progresses or what they will do. It is entirely up to the individual and their passing circumstances that will dictate how their spiritual development will unfold.

Suicides have a different path than a natural passing. Their path still requires earthly interaction.

Teresa to Angela: Come back in a few months. Michelle needs time to acclimate to her new home and environment. For both of you, this is too new. Both of you need time to heal.

It is not a rite of passage, when we pass over, to adjust quickly to **HEAVEN.** When you leave this earth, you leave this body and move into your **SPIRITUAL** body, which means an entirely new way of living. Moving from one consciousness to another consciousness is a new reality. It takes time for both of you to come to terms with a new way of life.

Teresa to Angela: Most people, when passing over to the **HEAVENS,** meet family, friends and their **GUARDIAN ANGELS.** There is a party on the other side, celebrating your new birthday back into eternal life. You have the ability to visit with your **SPIRITUAL** family, and then you go into the Healing hospital to heal and work on yourself. It takes time, and for every person it is different. However, for suicides there is a special place for them to get the help they need. We will talk further at your next appointment when you are feeling better as well.

The grieving process for parents whose children commit suicide can be extremely difficult, especially in seeking the answers. The guilt carried by the family can be burdensome. Yet, there is a connection that is unbreakable between a child and his or her parents. They feel our love and they know our pain. I suggested that Angela seek out grief counseling and personal therapy and that I would see her in a few months. Both Michelle and Angela will have had the time and proper assistance to help heal.

As a spiritual messenger and healer, I have been blessed and gifted to work with an amazing spiritual team which I refer to as my **TAG TEAM.**

Through their guidance and support, I have the ability to work on different levels in the **SPIRITUAL** realm.

I can communicate with loved ones, **ANGELS** and animals. I have been able to hear, see and feel **SPIRIT** since I was four years old and have been professionally reading for over 30 years. Quite often my **"TAG TEAM"** gives me the ability to view situations just as one watches a movie. I have the ability to pause, fast forward, rewind and compose all that information into a conversation for my clients.

During a reading, I can discuss a lot of information on all topics and all areas of concern. This has helped me to assist both the living and the deceased on their healing journey.

CHAPTER TWO
SO, WHY ARE YOU HERE?

*T*he complex and sometimes complicated web of life we weave starts before we are even born and interconnects us all through a **UNIVERSAL MASTER PLAN.** This **MASTER PLAN** involves each and every one of us to be our authentic, beautiful self, thereby contributing our unique life energies into the history of the universe.

The **UNIVERSAL MASTER PLAN** starts with your exclusive **LIFE CONTRACT.** Your distinct **LIFE CONTRACT** is all about who you are, who you will become and how all of that will happen.

Once you have decided to come back to Earth for another lifetime, if that's your belief, you and your **GUARDIAN ANGELS,** with the **CREATOR,** start designing your **LIFE CONTRACT.** This moving, breathing, living **CONTRACT** encompasses everybody you will ever encounter and everything that you will ever do. This includes your **SOUL GROUP** comprised of **SPIRITS** that have collectively decided to come, in body, with you to educate each other by sharing experiences. Our **SOUL GROUP** has been with us for many lifetimes. We all know each other and our interlacing experiences are essential in achieving the goals of our **CONTRACT.**

Living out your **LIFE CONTRACT** consists of complicated, overlapping layers containing many factors which include time, personality traits, desires, situations, issues and people. The **CONTRACT** is designed for all to participate in and agree to, helping each other to grow and experience life.

At various moments in life you are either the teacher, coaching the other people in your life with their lessons, or at other times you are the student learning from the many individuals who will come in and out of your life.

Some people stay for a moment, a day, a week, a month or a lifetime, depending on the contractual need of the lessons and how the symbiotic relationship unfolds. "Living a Life" is the specific reason you decided to come here. You chose to do this in order to grow your **SPIRIT'S** light through experiences and by helping others. In doing so, the collective consciousness of humanity's light shines brighter.

There are many questions that need to be answered before you are born. Some of them are:

How will your life start out? Who will be my parents?
What religion will I be? What nationally will I be?
What will my life be like? Why am I being born?
Who will I marry? Will I have children?
Will I be successful? Will I live a long life?
Who will I become?

Your **LIFE CONTRACT** begins with many pages about you. They include critical components that create the backbone of your **CONTRACT,** and everything else will become the supporting elements that comprise the essence of you and the details of your life. A divinely appointed network of connections is intertwined with your **CONTRACT** to provide the opportunity for all to benefit from life's education.

How will your life start out?

You decide the time and place you are going to be born. The time plays a large role in your personal development, for how the stars and planets align at the time of your birth, will forever in this lifetime have astrological significance. Each astrological sign provides certain qualities and information that will lend their energies to your life.

The place where you will be born denotes the geographic location that contributes to your spiritual evolution by providing cultural information as well as social indicators.

What will I look like?

You choose your name. This is extremely important. Your name has an energetic imprint, which plays a significant role on how your **SPIRIT** will live on Earth.

You choose your gender. The sexes provide specific experiences that are unique to the body you choose. You decide every element of your body including eye and hair color, height, weight and the overall appearance. You predetermine your nationality, which most often coincides with what you believe about **THE CREATOR.**

Everything you decide about your body, including health issues, will be part of helping you fulfill your life requirements. This code is then ingrained in your genetic composition through your DNA.

The direct correlation of your **LIFE PATH** and your genetic composition plays an important role in helping unfold your experiences and lessons to be learned. Within your body, experiences are being recorded through cellular memory, which is a component of our growth. Its energy kicks in when we learn lessons that change our reaction from a negative to a positive interaction, and it becomes an incorporated part of our whole being.

Growth then occurs, and we move into a new phase of our **LIFE CONTRACT. If growth does not take place, we keep repeating the same core is**sues. This determines your physical, mental and emotional health. Your overall well-being is a constant factor, which is taken into account in your spiritual development.

Who Am I?

Your personality characteristics are also predesigned by you. This is the core of how you will grow and develop. First you pick your personality traits, the things that will help and hurt your personal development. These traits are part of your **CORE SPIRIT** and are connected from lifetime to lifetime. Examples of these traits are a sense of humor, selfishness, generosity, quiescence, happiness, intelligence, stubbornness, compassion and forgiveness. If you are a person who holds a grudge, it will not help your soul to develop. If you are a person who has learned to forgive, then your development will proceed. It is all up to you as to how your development will advance. Your advancement will be a direct reflection of how you interact with people around you.

People are always watching and learning from you.

You and your **GUARDIAN ANGELS** choose your gifts from the **CREATOR.** There are core gifts that comprise your **SPIRIT.** Some of them are **LOVE, LIGHT,** compassion, peace, strength, sadness, courage, fear, anger and joy. Then there are specialty gifts such as the ability to sing, to write, to paint, to dance, to negotiate, to clean, to cook and to fight. Even though some traits may be viewed negatively, all are important because they provide an avenue by which we educate ourselves and those around us. Everyone's personality traits and gifts come in varying amounts, and you choose how much of each gift and trait you want. It is like going to a buffet restaurant where you get to pick how much or how little you want of each item. Each one of us has determined how we have chosen to evolve both physically and spiritually.

Through all the interactions with everyone involved in our lives we develop insight as to what lessons we need to learn and what lessons we can assist others to learn.

How do I define myself?

Our **CONTRACT** is ever changing and adapting to our earthly environment and influences, and they come to us from many different places, people and experiences.

We also decide what our interests and hobbies will be. Hobbies and interests are as varied as each individual and can range from mild to moderate to intense. Will you be a collector of dolls, memorabilia or historic items? Will your interests include knitting, photo scrapbooking or gemology? Will your hobbies include sports, outdoor adventures or travel? You may employ these interests to enrich your personal life or career.

What will my life be like?

You then move on to outlining your life challenges, opportunities, lessons and goals. These are not necessarily as time-sensitive as they are experience-driven.

Lessons come in at all stages of life.

Each stage of life affords us the opportunity to discover new aspects of ourselves. Through those challenges we get to see what we are really made of. The journey of self-discovery is a treasure chest buried deep inside of us, waiting to be unearthed.

Environmental factors can be a huge influence on how you shape yourself. However, the main factors that truly define your **SELF** are your faith and courage. Faith in yourself, faith that you have everything you need and the courage to use it. Then couple this with the Living Faith that there is a higher power that loves and desires to assist us.

Who will be in your life?

Before you arrive, you sit down with your **SOUL GROUP** at a collective community round table and decide who will play what role. You choose where in the sibling hierarchy you will be and what impact that will have on the family. You then collectively choose your parents, siblings, grandparents, extended family, friends, lovers, pets and future children.

Our immediate family paradigm is the first environmental factor that contributes to our **LIFE CONTRACT.** Our immediate family and their personalities contribute to our early childhood development and spiritual growth.

Included in the contract are earthly guardians there to provide love, support, protection and healing. These guardians most often are our pets. Animals have individual personalities and traits. Every unique animal contributes to our life experience and helps us to adhere to the lessons we have chosen to learn in this life.

Every person in our life is there for a reason.

As we grow older there will be many different people in life who help to support our journey and aid us in adhering to our contract.

How our lessons are learned.

Many people ask, "Why do bad things happen to good people?" This is an age-old question with a complex ripple effect.

Bad things need to happen so that we can learn to use the tools we are given to aid us in understanding our own internal voice.

The knowledge that our **SPIRIT** carries into this lifetime can only be accessed when it is called upon. When we are in difficult situations and things are not going well, we are required to muster qualities within ourselves to get the job done. If that situation did not present itself with difficulties, then we would not be able to go within and use our **GOD**-given gifts.

This reaction and interaction also allows others to follow the same process of understanding. Whether or not everybody involved interacts appropriately is not the goal. The goal is to accommodate each other's interaction and the exchange of information about how we react and grow.

Some people choose not to grow or develop. They will remain at the same level of spiritual evolution in this lifetime, as well as possibly many more.

The only thing for which we are responsible is our own growth, development and understanding. It may seem simple, but it takes a lifetime to become the master of our emotions.

This is part of the goal of living life here on Earth .

Our **LIFE CONTRACTS** are not exact or perfect. They are an outline of our quest and accomplishments. Our journey is not necessarily time-sensitive as much as it is experience driven. On the road of LIFE, we will pass what I call **MILE MARKERS** that are the situations in life that cannot be avoided and must be experienced.

Then there are what I refer to as **FLOATING FLAGS** that show up when unexpected human events present themselves. In your journey, there are times when the flags are invoked to protect and serve you for your highest good. These flags can be incorporated into your contract at a moment's notice.

There is one other factor, the unknown variable, **FREE WILL.**

Exercise of your **FREE WILL** also determines the practical application of your faith and will have influence on the faith of others around us. This has a domino effect on all contracts.

What we choose creates the next step in life. It creates what options will be next on our path as well as that of others. **FREE WILL** on the road of life is like the wind. It is that element that can cause a shift in direction.

Our **SPIRITUAL** family is influencing all of the adaptations in our **LIFE CONTRACT** from behind the scenes. As far as we know, it appears that we are in control. Nothing could be farther from the truth.

There are always signs, thoughts or ideas being sent into our consciousness to assist us in living life. What we choose to do with these things is part of our **FREE WILL,** but make no mistake, there are outside influences guiding us in a loving and positive direction. It does not make life any easier at the time, or change life's struggles, but there is always **LOVING LIGHT** being sent to help us.

The way it is explained to me via my **"TAG TEAM"** is that our **LIFE CONTRACT** has many layers, and depending on where we are in our life, what is needed for the highest good of ourselves and for the collective group, will be exactly how life unfolds.

We are exactly where we are supposed to be. There are no coincidences. When things go awry, it is the job of our **"TAG TEAM"** to help direct us to the correct path.

Nothing in our **LIFE CONTRACT** goes without the guidance of our **GUARDIAN ANGEL** and the **CREATOR'S** approval.

We all come into this life equipped with the tools necessary to fulfill our **LIFE CONTRACT**. However, there is no instruction manual. This is why we need each other's help. In order for us to execute our **LIFE CONTRACT** it requires participation from everyone, most importantly, ourselves.

Our **CONTRACT** is a codependent agreement between us and everyone else, and it is only successful if the people in our world are there to participate.

If one person decides that he or she no longer wants to live here on Earth and chooses to take his or her own life via suicide, it breaks the agreement.

When the agreement is broken, the domino effect is seen throughout all the **SOUL GROUP CONTRACTS**. The individual **CONTRACT** is broken but not forgotten. Their **CONTRACT** still has to be upheld for all the others in their group. The **GROUP CONTRACT** has to be implemented whether or not this individual is here on Earth or on the other side.

This is why suicides do not get to rest in peace and enjoy the loving luxury of the **LIGHT**. They will be allowed to be in the **LIGHT**, but their eternal life will forever be reconstructing their role in other people's **CONTRACTS**.

Since they took their lives, the void created in the Universe and the magnitude of damage will have to be assessed and addressed.

He or she will have to work hard from the other side to assist in implementing the events and situations that were supposed to unfold for each individual to whom their **CONTRACT** is connected. This is no easy task. It will take an entire **SPIRITUAL TEAM** to embark on repairing the damage that has been done to everyone.

This includes the people who were alive and actively involved in the life of the young adolescent prior to their death. But even more devestating, is the fact that this also has bearing on the youth's future offspring. Removing themselves from the **SOUL GROUP CONTRACT** removes their progeny, as well as any other future family connections for which he or she might have been responsible.

It also changes the course of history, for if they themselves were destined to change their family, society or the world, that could not now be recreated. If their children were destined to create, develop, or impact the world in an unprecedented way, that also would never happen.

Since each one of us is an individual, unique **SPIRITUAL** being having a **CONTRACT** to help, it is imperative that we do our part to fulfill the agreement. There are no substitutes for any of us.

If we do not fulfill what we came here to do, then it doesn't get accomplished, and there is no one in the future to take our place.

The results of this one act will forever have a catastrophic impact on humanity.

Suicide victims will review their **LIFE CONTRACT** and be schooled on how to correct and reconstruct other people's lives so that whatever interaction he/she was supposed to provide still occurs. However, the permanent damage to their potential spouses and their offspring will forever have cataclysmic results.

The act of taking your own life, no matter what the reason, destroys help and hope for the future of the world, ultimately devastating the ability for the **UNIVERSAL MASTER PLAN** to unfold.

CHAPTER THREE
TAG YOU'RE IT!

*M*y work is a blessing in many ways.

Through the gifts I have been given, my clients are able to heal by finding closure, understanding, clarity and peace as I reconnect them with their loved ones. My passion for people in need and animals, has always tugged at my heart. Being a medium was not the path I intended. I wanted to be a Veterinarian specializing in large animals.

When I was four years old, I first spoke of **SPIRITS** at a family gathering. As I grew up, I became aware of ANGELS all around me, interrelating within my environment. My first formal introduction to my spiritual family, who I fondly refer to as my **"TAG TEAM,"** was when I was in my twenties. They came to me after a paranormal experience and have been visibly present every moment of everyday of my life.

Every person has a spiritual family consisting of a **"TAG TEAM,"** which stands for **"TEACHERS, ANGELS AND GUIDES."** Their job is to be your supportive SPIRITUAL family in just the same way as we are born here into a family consisting of a mother, father, siblings and extended family, including grandparents, aunts, uncles and cousins. We also have that similar arrangement and connection with **SPIRIT.**

My anagram for this beautiful family is, **"TAG TEAM."**

There is a **CORE "TAG TEAM"** that has been with you since the day you were born, and there are also **SPECIALISTS** who are brought in to assist when you are in a life situation with which your **CORE TEAM** needs help. Each member of the team has a specific purpose.

We all have come to Earth to share our blessings so that our **SPIRIT** can evolve through life experiences. With each new experience there is a lesson to be learned. If we learn our lesson, then we move forward, but if we do not, we repeat the lesson over and over until the lesson is learned.

Your **TEACHERS** on the other side are there to assist you with life lessons. Their job is to ensure that the lessons you have written in to your **LIFE CONTRACT are implemented. It is up to you as to whether or no**t you will grow and develop. These **TEACHERS** will make every effort to follow through with their responsibilities. They have had at least one earthly life and have lived at least one earthly life _with you, either in this life or a past life._

You do know them from other past lives.

They have chosen to stay in **SPIRIT** to assist you. While helping you they share in the opportunity to evolve their own **SPIRIT.** It is a mutually beneficial arrangement.

Your **GUIDES'** responsibilities are very similar to that of being teachers, but their "job description" is slightly different. Their responsibility is to help you deal with your emotions as they help guide you through life's emotional heartache and pain. They also revel in the happiness and joy of your successes.

Your **ANGELS** are the glue that keeps the family together, for they are a gift from **THE CREATOR.** They know how to work the **SPIRITUAL** realm, for they have been there since the beginning of time. They are your **"GO TO" SPIRITS.** They have never been here on Earth in human form, so they rely on the Teachers and Guides who have had earthly life experiences, to be here to guide, support and help provide you a well-rounded team effort.

ANGELS provide a unique energy to every situation. They are the guiding energy and light that make things happen. Opening up your heart and mind to allow them in will allow you to feel comforted and supported during your life.

If your core **"TAG TEAM"** cannot help you, they will go out and seek **SPECIALISTS** who are the best at working with you to help in your time of need. There are specialists from every heavenly realm that are there to assist the living with the complicated situations of life.

You are never alone. They are always present and helping you. You might not notice them, but they are hard at work behind the scenes.

Your GUARDIAN ANGEL is not part of your "TAG TEAM."

Your **GUARDIAN ANGELS** are your **SPIRITUAL PARENTS.** Their job as your **SPIRITUAL PARENT** is to help you by connecting through your consciousness and accessing your inner voice. They have been with you since the beginning of your **SPIRITUAL** birth in the Heavens. They are part of your "internal GPS system", helping you navigate life. This vital bond establishes a bridge of **LIGHT** revealing and opening up the highway to a bigger plan.

It is vital for all of us to participate in a Master Plan.

Your **GUARDIAN ANGELS** are aware of the plan and will help you execute your **LIFE CONTRACT.** They are constantly leaving you visible signs in your daily life like a trail of bread crumbs.

They have the ability to influence people and situations through their positive energetic connection. They can put people in your life who provide critical information, thereby helping you navigate through the journey of life.

There are no coincidences in this life - your vigilant **"TAG TEAM"** has your back. Your road may not be easy, there may be potholes, construction or closures, but there will always be a **SPIRITUAL** family member redirecting your course.

You entire **"TAG TEAM"** and **ANGELS** wish to be invited into your life by a simple request. Their sole purpose for being is to lovingly live for you. This requires awareness on your part that you do have **SPIRITUAL** family and friends.

You can use any form of invitation that you desire.

Some people like to verbalize in the form of prayers, and some people simply like to write down their prayers. Some people like to ask or demand - it does not matter how you call upon them. All they ask is that you call on them!! They are there, regardless, whether you call for them or not, BUT calling for them opens an energy field for their enraptured love to envelope your world.

Many people often express their unhappiness in that they feel they cannot connect with their **GUARDIAN ANGEL** or **"TAG TEAM."** What I am given to tell you is that they rarely speak in loud, audible voices - their work is through infinite loving energy.

They might work by sending you a thought or an idea that just pops in your head.

Sometimes they use physical signs,a feather, the lights dimming or even small objects such as pennies, as ways to get your attention. Many times, they use other people as messengers to deliver what they want you to know.

What you must understand is that there is a higher power and a plan that is greater than us, and it contains all the information about you and your life.

It does not matter in what religion you worship, and it doesn't matter what belief system you have or what part of the world you are born in or in what culture you exist. Every person born on this planet has a core **"TAG TEAM"** and a **GUARDIAN ANGEL** assigned to him or her for the duration of their earthly life. Some people may even have more than one **GUARDIAN ANGEL**.

Everybody's path is uniquely beautiful and different.
We all have a contract and need to abide by
the spiritual agreement.

CHAPTER FOUR
ANGELA WANTS ANSWERS

*I*t has been six months since I last sat down with Angela to talk with Michelle.

Angela sits down, I take her hands and I do my traditional opening, when she stops me immediately and asks...

Angela: Do you think Michelle will talk to me about her death?

Teresa: I have not opened up the connection yet, and I will not know until the door opens. I do a trinity connection that consists of my energy, her energy and **THE CREATOR'S**. Once I establish my divine spiritual link, I will be able to talk with whoever is waiting to communicate with you.

For some reason I do not recognize Angela, and she looks only vaguely familiar

Teresa: Have I read you before?

Angela looks at me with a puzzled look on her face.

Angela: Yes, you have read me before. Don't you remember me and what happened last time?

Teresa: I am so sorry. It might seem odd to you, but I do not remember you. Once you leave my office, your reading dissolves, and your family member leaves with you.

I am only a conduit for **SPIRIT'S** communication, and I pass the information along as I receive it. That is the reason I record every session so that you can refer back to the conversation. I do not retain any information from our session. Even if you called me five minutes after the reading ended to ask me a question, I would not be able to give you any answers. It is not my information to retain, but rather yours to keep, to help you understand and heal.

I explain to her that I see so many clients, and do so many personal readings, public events, house parties and the like, that I cannot physically remember everybody I have spoken with. My explanation settles Angela down, and I proceed to go to work.

I take a deep breath (as I usually do) and the **DIVINE LIGHTED DOOR** opens. The first **SPIRIT** to greet me is an ANGEL who is smiling at me. He takes my hand and tells me we are all ready. I reply, "Thank you."

My first connection is with Angela's father. He tells me he has an unusual name that sounds like "wha," but I also get the letter "J," so I repeat this to her.

Angela: My father's name was Joaquim.

Teresa: Thanks. He tells me that he left too early from a heart attack, and he saw you grow up from a teenager into a lovely woman.

Teresa: He says he is sorry, and he should've taken better care of himself. He knew that heart disease ran in his family. He tells me that his father and two brothers also died early in life from heart attacks. He wishes he could have been there for your wedding, but he did walk with you down the aisle and was present the whole time.

Teresa to Joaquim: Is there something you could tell me to prove to Angela that you were there at her wedding?

Joaquim: While Angela was getting dressed her zipper jammed, and they could not get the dress zipped up all the way.

I relay this information to Angela

Angela: Yes! My Aunt was a seamstress, and she was able to fix the zipper.

Teresa: He also tells me that as you were waiting to walk down the aisle, one of the roses fell out of your bouquet. He says he pulled it out to let your know that he was there. He had a small rose garden in his yard, he loved to garden and he wanted this to be a sign from him.

As I am relaying this information from her father to her, I see a tear streaming down her face.

Teresa: Is the information that I am being given correct?

Angela: Yes, but I did not know that it was my father pulling out the rose from the bouquet. I could not understand how it happened because the arrangement was so tightly put together. My brother who walked me down the aisle even commented on how strange that was. It now all makes sense. He loved to garden, and he had all types of flowers.

Angela's father tells me that roses were his favorite, and as a sign from him he sends her the smell of roses.

Teresa: Your dad tells me that the smell of flowers, especially roses, is a sign from him.

Angela: I most often smell roses when I am in the kitchen looking out the window into my back yard or while I'm driving.

While I am talking with Angela, her dad fills my room with a beautiful, fragrant flower aroma. It gets so strong that I have to tell Joaquim to tone it down. He does.

Angela: How does this happen?

Teresa: The longer you are in **SPIRIT,** the more you learn to live in **SPIRIT.** There are so many things that you learn. One is how to manifest smells, objects and manipulate the physical realm, such as flickering lights.

They do this in order to let us folks here on earth know that they are with us.

Teresa: Your father tells me that he is still smoking and drinking his coffee, just like he did while he was here.

Angela acts surprised.

Teresa: You can do anything you want when you are in **SPIRIT.** **HEAVEN** is what you make it. If you believe that you will drink coffee, read the paper and watch the news, then that is exactly what you will do.

I have spoken with many **SPIRITS** telling me that they are playing bingo, cards, living in a beautiful house or even just sitting looking out a window. Some tell me that they have jobs and work to help us here on earth.

SPIRIT wants to make **HEAVEN** fit your belief structure so that you adjust comfortably.

Her dad says that he loves her and will continue to watch over her and send her signs of love so she knows that he is present in her life. He then steps back out of my view, which means somebody else is going to step forward.

Angela's mom steps in next and she tells me that she has been there a shorter time than her husband. She asks Angela why she is not wearing her jewelry. I get a sense that this is very important to her mom.

Teresa: Why are you not wearing your mom's jewelry?

Angela's facial expression changes, and I can see her aura changed as well. It went from bright colors to a dimmed pale gray. This is not a good sign.

Angela: I have no room for it.

Angela's Mom: Yes, you could have worn my pearl necklace it would go well with that shirt.

By the way this conversation was going I could tell - with my "**TAG TEAM'S**" assistance - that the relationship between Angela and her mother was a strained one, at best.

Teresa: My "**TAG TEAM**" tells me that your mom is all about appearances - how she physically looked and what would the neighbors think.

Angela rolls her eyes.

Angela: That's my Mom!

As I start to make a point, Angela's mom continues to attempt to control our conversation. As I try to talk with Angela, her mom begins to speak even louder from the other side.

Her mom is a very stubborn and determined angry **SPIRIT** who constantly pushes to get her way.

I continue to explain to her that personalities transcend time; therefore, how a person behaved here on Earth is how they are going to behave on the other side. Their memories, belief and attitude structures are part of their SPIRIT'S composition.

Angela (Laughing): I know all about my mom! Tell her I forgive her, I love her and I knew what she was all about, but could we please move on.

Angela's mom is not happy with the way this conversation went and starts yelling at me, demanding that she wanted "her time".

As a result of doing this work for so long, I knew that this conversation was not going to go well. So, I had already preemptively called in my "**TAG TEAM**" and some others for support to take

Angela's mother out of my connection. They were way ahead of me, as their loving energy gently pulled her away and guided her into the light.

When a situation like this develops, I find it is best to let the client decide whether they want to continue to talk to that family member.

I take a moment and recompose the energy in the room. I ask who would like to talk next. I see many people around Angela. In the way I work spiritually, my **"TAG TEAM"** puts a visual microphone in front of me, and each **SPIRIT** in my perimeter is allowed to come closer and talk into the microphone. This allows only one **SPIRIT** at a time to talk, avoiding the confusion that can occur when several **SPIRITS** talk all at the same time.

When there are too many **SPIRITS** talking all at once the information becomes convoluted, confusing and diluted. I wait …

I hear jingling.

I wait to connect with this person, and I see a young woman approach, and she gives me what I refer to as my "daughter sign".

Teresa: I have your daughter here.

Angela: Michelle.

Michelle steps forward and gives me a big hug, then turns to her mom and envelops her with beautiful pink energy, giving her mom a beautiful embrace. I notice that Angela must have felt it because she immediately relaxes, a peaceful look comes over her, and she smiles.

Michelle: My mom is doing much better and has gotten more comfortable with what has happened.

Angela to Teresa: Ask Michelle to tell you about her passing.

Michelle responds immediately.

Michelle: When I passed, I met Nan, Pop-Pop and Boomer.

Boomer jumps right up on my lap and licks my face. I tell Angela what Michelle said, and also that Boomer is sitting on my lap. She tells me that Boomer loved to jump up and lick everyone. I put Boomer down so I can talk with Michelle.

She tells me all about her life on the other side and how she spends time with her spiritual family, learning how to live in HEAVEN. I relay this to Angela.

Angela: Ask Michelle to talk about the suicide.

Michelle agrees she is now ready.

Teresa: What happened?

 Michelle makes me feel relaxed and sends a wind in my face, **followed by LIGHT.**

**That light is The Light of Heaven.** I have experienced it many times before while working.

Teresa to Angela: Michelle made me feel as if there was wind in her face before she passes.

Angela: Don't you remember that she jumped off the building?

Teresa: No, I do not remember.

Michelle: Tell my mom that I am sorry for all the pain I caused. Ask Mom if she read the notes I left for her and Dad.

Teresa to Angela: Michelle is telling me about the notes she left for you and her dad, as well as the holiday gifts that she had already bought. Did you get all of them?

Michelle: Tell her I meant every word in my note.

Mom, I love you and Dad. I did not want to disappoint you.

Teresa to Michelle: What was going on with you?

College, I got depressed and had a hard time adjusting to college life. I concealed it from everybody. I could not deal with showing them that I was not perfect. Outwardly, I continued to smile and laugh but I felt like I didn't fit in. I had a hard time making real friends. It was just so different from high school, and I felt like I was constantly playing catch up with my course requirements. In high school I studied, but not a lot, and the information came easy.

Here at college, I felt overwhelmed with the amount of material. The things I loved to do in high school, like writing (I wrote for the school newspaper). I was not able to do at college. I was not chosen to write for the newspaper at college. I did not understand why and that also got me very upset, and that was one of the factors that started my self-doubt.

There were other students that were smarter than me, better writers and they did not struggle the way I did to maintain good grades. I received a softball scholarship and I was a great athlete. I was not only a softball player, but I was also on the track team. I loved to run. In college, the competition and pressure was far greater than I expected. I wasn't doing as well in sports as I did in high school. I didn't make the first team.

Teresa: You are only a freshman, why would you think you would make the first team?

Michelle: In high school, when I was a freshman I made the varsity team. I was recruited early from college and I thought I was the best. Everybody told me I was the best! In high school I was always top in the game, doing my best to be the best!

She shows me my signs for "no alcohol and drugs" and lets me know she gave me those signs because she "did not do those things." She was having a hard time fitting into the scene.

I explain all of this to Angela.

Angela: The last time Michelle was home she seemed different. She kept more to herself. She looked tired and was not happy. I did ask her what was wrong, and she told me that everything was good, and that she was just tired.

Angela went on to tell me that she pressured Michelle on this topic in other conversations that weekend because she said she could see something was not right.

Michelle, at one point, did ask Angela what she would think if she did not go back to college. Angela said that she continued to ask Michelle to tell her what was really going on. She told me that Michelle just backed off from the conversation, and said that it was just a silly, passing thought.

Angela tells me that she feels extremely guilty for not forcing Michelle to reveal what was going on.

Michelle tells me to tell this her mother:

Michelle: (in a determined voice) MOM, IT IS NOT YOUR FAULT! PLEASE DO NOT FEEL GUILTY!! THERE IS NO WAY YOU COULD HAVE KNOWN! I DID NOT TELL ANYONE.

Teresa to Michelle: Why?

Michelle (in a childlike manner): I made mistakes. I did not want my family to think I could not handle it. I did not want them to be disappointed in me. I was not making good grades. I was not playing good ball. I kept making mistakes. I missed my friends and my life back home.

Teresa to Angela: Michelle was having a difficult time being in a strange world with no skills to cope with the pressure and stress of college life.

Angela: I don't understand. My daughter was a success in high school, and she was loved by everyone and always did well!

Michelle to Teresa: Tell my mom I did not even know how to tell her what I was feeling. Everything was just spinning faster and faster! I felt like everything was slipping away! I did not know who I was or what I was doing here at college! I felt like there was no hope!

With this, Michelle's **Guardian Angel** wraps her in blue loving light and they both step back.

The **ANGELS** step in at that moment and tell me to tell Angela that she did a great job raising her daughter and she should be proud of her for all that she did accomplish.

I tell her.

Then I need to tell her the truth.

I ask the **ANGELS** for help delivering a different perspective on the situation. To a grieving mother, especially, this kind of information is always extremely difficult.

I take a deep breath and ask the **ANGELS** to give me the best way to deliver this information to Angela - in a way in which she could receive and understand it without taking on more guilt.

Teresa to Angela: Do you recall anytime in your daughter's life that she did not succeed in the things in which she put her mind and effort?

Angela: No. Michelle has always been successful. I never had any problems with her, she did her homework, she played sports, she wrote for the paper and she had a lot of friends. Everybody looked up to her, and we were all proud of her.

Teresa: Did your daughter know what it felt like to not be a success? Did she know what it was like to be average or "just good"?

Angela pauses for a moment.

Angela: I don't know. I guess not. She always did everything with ease. Things seemed to come easy for her. Not like her sisters who had to work very hard.

I then proceed to explain, as the **ANGELS** show me, that Michelle was a big deal in her community - kind of like - and I actually said, "Excuse the cheesy analogy - but a beautiful, big fish in a small pond where everybody gives her praise and accolades. Then she goes off to college where she is no longer viewed and admired as such. She is now a big fish in an ocean where she has to establish herself in an unfamiliar setting, with little or no support, not having people to encourage her."

Teresa: Do you understand what I just explained?

Angela: This is the first time I had ever thought of it that way. I always saw my daughter as well balanced and stable.

The **ANGELS** explained that while she was here at home, Michelle had a community, friends and family always encouraging her and supporting everything she did. She constructed her view of herself and her private world based on what she perceived other people's eyes were seeing. Now that she was on her own in an unfamiliar environment, with nobody supporting her, she needed, every day, to rely on her own self-confidence, internal fortitude and trust that she was making good decisions. She had never had to do that before, and it became so overwhelming that her own self-identity began to breakdown, and she spiraled down into depression.

Feeling no way out, she got caught up in the constant pain and torture of seeing herself become a failure. The **ANGELS** explain that her actions are not condoned or in compliance with the spiritual laws.

They wanted me to share this information with you so that you, as well as your husband, would stop beating yourselves up, and stop taking on the responsibility for Michelle's death. You have two other children to attend to, and they need your love, support and presence. Being totally pre-occupied with Michelle's death is causing your girls to raise themselves without your interaction and love.

There is a break in the conversation and Michelle steps forward. She asks me to tell her mom, in a very determined tone:

I LOVE YOU AND DAD. YOU WERE THE BEST PARENTS. I AM SORRY. PLEASE, PLEASE FORGIVE ME."

I tell Angela everything, including that Michelle is asking for forgiveness.

Angela (stunned and still angry): If you did not commit suicide, I would not have to forgive you. If you were here I could hold you and tell you everything is going to be ok.

Michelle asks me to tell her mom that she did not know where to turn,**"I AM SORRY, MOM. PLEASE FORGIVE ME!!"**

Angela: You could have called me or your father. You could have called the campus help line, called anyone!!!

Michelle: I was the one always helping everybody else, I did not know how. Mom, I need for you to forgive me, PLEASE!!

Angela, still deeply grieving, needs more time.

Teresa to Michelle: Your mom needs more time. For her, it is still too soon.

I can see the **ANGELS** interceding, and the energy in the room becomes calm and relaxed. The **ANGELS** tell me that Michelle understands.

Angela, who is still hurting, continues to cry uncontrollably. I see Michelle hug her mother, and she gives me a wink and tells me, "I will talk to you again soon."

I thought that was an odd message from Michelle. That does not happen. I shrugged it off and turned my attention to back to Angela and the reading.

At that point everybody steps out of my view and the door closes. I thanked everybody for assisting in our conversation. Only Love and **LIGHT** remain.

Readings, for the most part, are emotionally draining, and suicides are especially both physically and emotionally depleting for me. It takes all of what is left of my available energy to conclude our time together.

Teresa: Angela, forgiveness is a bridge where both of you will meet again and find a way to love again.

Angela: I cannot forgive her.

I explain to her that this is all still to raw and that the grieving process for everyone is different. I tell her to take her time and continue to get the counseling and help she and her family needs.

As she regains her composure, I reiterate that the information that the **ANGELS** gave her was very deep. I ask Angela if she understands what I have explained to her from an **ANGELIC** perspective. Angela looks very puzzled and confused. She tells me this is a lot for her to take in, and that she will need some time to think about all of this.

I agree.

Angela stayed in her seat for a several minutes composing her thoughts, and I could see that she was trying to wrap her head around everything we had just discussed.

After a while, I asked her if she was ok, and would she like a glass of water. She snapped out of her thoughts looked at me directly in my eyes and said, "Thank you."

I was taken aback. I was not sure how she took the news. I often get so caught up with my spiritual conversations that I have a difficult time gauging my client's perceptions. She was happy that her daughter was not alone and that she was with her grandparents. That information made her feel comforted.

She said she felt a sense of peace and even a little relieved that she now had a better understanding of what happened. It would take her some time, but she was glad we had recorded it so she could listen to it again. She asked me if she could she let her husband and children listen to our session.

I explained that this was her information, and she may do as she likes with it. She said that she had hopes that it will help all of them, and that it might even bring them closer together. She stood up, and I gave her a big hug and told her that my door was open when she wanted to talk again.

Even though Angela left my office, I had a feeling this was not the end of this reading. The way that Michelle ended our conversation, winking at me, telling me that she will "talk to me again soon," had never ever happened in my career up to that point.

I asked my **"TAG TEAM"** if they have any insight for me of what she was referring to, and their response was, "There is more to come." I took it to mean that Angela would be back, soon, for another reading.

I did not know it at the time, but that was not entirely the correct interpretation.

At the end of day I close the **DIVINE LIGHTED DOOR** and thank everybody for joining me to help those in need. Closing the day requires a specific routine that I follow to ensure that everybody is safe and protected.

CHAPTER FIVE
THE GANG IS ALL HERE!

*K*nock......
*K*nock......

I look over to the clock and it is 2:22 a.m. I pull the covers back over my head, and I hear an even louder **'KNOCK KNOCK'** on my bedroom door.

I say out loud, "Hey, I worked all day yesterday and worked last night helping people pass over, and I'm tired. I don't want to work another night."

For a few brief moments it's quiet.

Now I feel something poking me through the blankets, and I know it's my **GUARDIAN ANGEL** because she is the only one allowed in my room while I'm sleeping.

My rule is: when I work at night (which I do often), any **SPIRITS** that are in need of help adjusting to their passing must keep a distance, as my only sanctuary is my bedroom.

GUARDIAN ANGEL: They're here!

Teresa (pulling the covers back): Who's here? When we worked in the past you've never said, "They're here!!"

GUARDIAN ANGEL: You have to get up. They want to talk to you.

Teresa (in my unique, smartass way): Really, I got to get up? Can't we do this tomorrow?

GUARDIAN ANGEL: No, get up.

I peer over towards the threshold of my bedroom, and there are so many **SPIRITS** smiling and waving excitedly looking at me.

Teresa: Who are they? What do they want?

GUARDIAN ANGEL (very gently and sweetly): They have heard that you are writing a book about teenage suicide. They are here to help you write your book. They want to be part of the book by telling you their life stories.

Resolved that I am destined to get no sleep tonight, I get out of bed, put my robe on and walk out of my bedroom into the hallway. All the loving energy I feel makes me cry.

I compose myself and the first **SPIRIT** that steps forward looks vaguely familiar to me.

I've seen her before. As I'm trying to wrap my head around all of this, she steps forward, and she hugs me. I realize it's Michelle.

Teresa: What are you doing here with all these people?

Michelle: I've been working on the other side telling everybody that you're writing a book, and they want to help.

With this, every **SPIRIT** says in unison _**"We want to tell our stories."**_

This completely takes me aback.

Teresa: Michelle, what have you been telling them?

54

Michelle: The ANGELS and everybody here know when we were in a reading with you we can't tell everything we know because it's too much for our parents to handle emotionally. We can't tell them everything we want them to know, and there is so much more to tell them than what is given in the readings.

Teresa: What do you mean?

Michelle: We want to talk about what goes on here after we pass. We want others to know what our eternal life is like.

Teresa: I know from all the work I do that passings are much more complex. There is so much more in the HEAVENS that goes on that so many people don't even know.

Michelle: Exactly, that is why we want to help you write the book.

I look around and I see many young SPIRITS, many of which I've never met before, and a few which I have, and they introduce themselves to me one by one.

As I look around I ask everybody...

Teresa: Do you want me to tell your stories and all your personal details?

Every SINGLE SPIRIT in my hall way responds with an overwhelming, "YES."

One young girl steps forward. She is about 11 years old. Her name is Britney, and she gives me a big hug.

Britney: Can you call my Mommy to tell her I'm OK?

Teresa: I've never met you, and I do not think I have spoken to your mom.

Britney: No, my mom doesn't believe. I send her signs that I am with her. Please call my mom.

Teresa: How can I call her?

Britney: There were a lot of articles written about me in the paper.

Teresa: That's not the way I work. I cannot reach out to her. That goes against the spiritual principles I live by. But I can help.

I turn to my **GUARDIAN ANGEL** and **"TAG TEAM"** and ask them to get Britney's Mom help in only the way that they can. They nod, and I know that they will work on it.

As Britney steps back, everybody floods me with love, joy and happiness. Everybody starts to talk all at once, sending me images, signs, smells and thoughts. I feel very overwhelmed so I step back into my bedroom, my sanctuary. I take a deep breath.

Teresa: There need to be some guidelines for us working together. The first guideline is one person at a time. Second, you can't all talk at the same time. You can all hang together while I'm interviewing each person, but there cannot be any crosstalk. Third, there cannot be any interruption in my daily life. You guys cannot interfere with other people's readings.

Teresa: Fourth, we cannot do this every night. I have to get some sleep and rest.

I turned to my Guardian Angels and my **"TAG TEAM"** and asked them if they agree. Everyone agrees and smiles.

Teresa: How are we going to handle the other private work that I do at night, helping loved ones who passed and are having difficulty transitioning into the light?

"TAG TEAM:" We will find another way while you do this work.

Feeling extremely exhausted, but excited, I ask who will be my first interview. Michelle steps forward and wants to be the first, so we arrange to start the process, later, in a few nights. Since there is no time on the other side, I will let them know when I am ready to stay up and work through the night.

For days I gave this a lot of thought. I was worried about how I could do this. There are so many **SPIRITS** who want to tell their stories. How am I going to put it all in one book??!! While I was in the shower this morning, my **"TAG TEAM"** comes to me and asks me why I am worrying? I immediately interrupt them, "Are you kidding me, there are so many **SPIRITS!!** I don't know if I can do this!!"

My **GUARDIAN ANGEL** sweetly steps in and says, "You have been working on this all of your life. You have done the personal work, and you have been doing the professional work for over 30 years. You are ready, and we have never let you down."

Know that this is true of **ANGELS;** they only speak the truth. I concede and tell them, "I am still worried, but I have faith and trust that with your help this will happen. But, I need help." They reply, "You can do this. You have tools. We will use all of your gifts to make this go smoothly." I tell them, "Let's make sure the electronic devices do not blow up. Every time I embark on this type of work, the energy takes down the equipment. Phones, computers and video equipment all get affected. I will need all that to get this done."

Their response is, "Don't worry." I am saying to myself, "Really, last time I had to buy a new cell phone." Shaking my head trying to finish showering, I feel the energy change, and the hot shower now turns cold. In their usual fashion working with me, they need to sometimes shock me into reality. It's in these moments that I tell myself to get a grip!

As a Spiritual Communicator, I know that **SPIRITS** have no physical bodies while in **HEAVEN,** and all of the communication is done through telepathic knowing. For the context of human understanding, I am told to write the book as if there is a physical, audible conversation, in order to help facilitate the truth and understanding of the heavenly realms.

Several nights later, as I have gotten a few nights sleep, I tell my **"TAG TEAM"** that I am ready to start the interviews. They let me sleep for a couple of hours and, again, I am woken up at 2:22 a.m.

Michelle is waiting at my threshold. I get up, grab my cell phone so I can record what I am about to channel, and begin my discussion with Michelle. I use my cell phone to record myself speaking the words I am given.

Teresa: Michelle, what was your life like before you left?

Michelle: It was a good life. When I was younger, I was very involved in dance and karate and having play dates with my friends. I was always very active, and as I got older I was more involved in school activities. I was part of the Drama Club, student government and I was an athlete. I loved track, softball and volleyball. I liked to write. I had dreams of traveling to other countries through my sports and writing.

She shows me that she spent a lot of time on her phone texting and checking social media. She says she did not spend a lot of time at home because, by the time they got home from practices, games or events, it was usually late.

Teresa: When did you have time to do your homework?

Michelle : I did a lot of it at school, while my parents were driving or before class.

Teresa: How was school for you?

Michelle: It was a breeze.

I allow her to talk, and she does so quickly and full of enthusiasm. She tells me about her family life and that she had two younger sisters, Maria and Monica. She was closer to Maria than Monica. She tells me that she gave Monica a hard time, often making fun of her and it would turn into an argument or a fight. She hung out with them while she was at home, but she didn't spend a lot of time at home. She was always busy with her activities.

Teresa: How often did you and your family sit and have dinner together or just hang out?

Michelle: Maybe on the weekends, but most of the time Mom and Dad were driving us to different events.

Teresa: Were your sisters involved in many activities as well?

Michelle: Yes, that's why we are always on the road.

Teresa: So when did you guys get time to sit as a family and talk?

Michelle: We would catch up usually around the center island in the kitchen once in a while or before we went to bed, but we also talked while Mom or Dad was driving.

Teresa: What did you talk about?

Michelle: We talked about the usual stuff: how I did in school, my sports, my sisters, how they did in school, their sports, their activities, normal stuff like that.

Teresa: Did you ever talk about how you felt about things that you found challenging or difficult?

Michelle: I never really did because nothing ever really was difficult, and if anything was a problem Mom or Dad handled it.

Teresa: Why did you give Monica a hard time?

Michelle: She was always in my stuff! Once she read my diary, and I freaked out screaming and yelling. She wasn't like me and Maria. Monica did not like sports, dancing or anything athletic.

Teresa: What did she like to do?

Michelle: She was always coloring and drawing. She would make funny pictures of me, and it made me mad.

Teresa: What did your parents do when you gave Monica a hard time?

Michelle: They would separate us. My mom usually took her side, and I would just go to my room. Sometimes my dad would come into my room and tell me not to worry, it will all work out.

Teresa: Did you ever talk to Monica and ask her why?

Michele tells me that she regrets the way she was with her sister, but she really never had a sisterly conversation with her.

Teresa: Were any of your friends 'like a sister,' that you were close with?

Michelle: In high school there were a few of us who were good friends. We would go to the mall, each other's houses and text a lot.

Teresa: When you had difficulties with your friends how did you handle it?

Michelle: There were not really any difficulties.

Teresa: Did any of them go to college with you?

Michelle: No!!

Teresa: Did you have any boyfriends in high school?

Michelle: I had a crush on one boy and hung out with another, but he was more like a brother.

Teresa: Were you close to any of your extended family?

Michelle: I was close to my aunt, my mom's sister.

Teresa: How close were you? Could you call her if you were having problems?

Michelle: I guess so.

Teresa: Did you reach out to her when you were having problems in college?

Michelle: No.

Teresa: Why not?

Michelle (in a frustrating tone): I could not. I did not want it to get back to my parents. I thought I could handle it.

Teresa: Was there anything about your life that you would change?

After a long pause she said...

Michelle: I would not have taken my life.

Teresa: Tell me about your time just before you took your own life.

Michelle: Quite a few things happened to me before getting to the top of the building.

I am shown a series of events that happened before her last day.

Days before, she had run into one of her old teachers from high school who was taking his son to visit the school, and they stopped and spoke for a while. They talked about how she was missed at home and how proud he was of her and her scholarships.

He said to her what a coincidence it was that he ran into her on such a large campus. She shrugged it off and told him to have a good visit.

Another time she was going to her dorm room, and a dog ran up to her that looked just like Boomer and wanted to play with her. The dog jumped up on her and licked her face. She looked around and she did not see any owner. She pet the dog rubbing his belly just the same way she did with Boomer. She got distracted by a person entering the dorm and turned around and the dog was gone.

She didn't even miss a beat, and she opened the door and proceeded to walk up the stairs to her room, never giving it a thought.

One day, while putting some of her stuff away, she saw a picture fall out of her notebook. She picked it up and it was of her and her family at their shore house. Everyone was happy. She stared at the picture for a long time then put it away.

While she was shopping, she met a woman in the store who spoke to her, unsolicited, and said, "Honey, don't worry. You have your whole life ahead of you."

I watch her, and she seems to be preoccupied.

She told me for many days prior to her making her final decision she spent a long time writing letters to her family. She even went out and purchased gifts. During that time she said she would smell flowers, and most often the smell of roses. There were times that it would permeate her whole dorm room.

Teresa: Did you not notice that there were many things in your way trying to get you to reconsider your decision?

Michelle: At the time my only focus was my own pain and, I wanted to accomplish everything before the end of the semester.

Teresa: What was the urgency for the deadline?

Michelle: I could not have my grades released.

Michelle: I didn't want to be exposed. I couldn't keep up with school, softball and a social life. I did not finish my papers. I did not want anybody to find out that I was a failure. I was afraid and desperate.

Teresa: Why didn't you get help?

Michelle: The depression and fear made everything feel so overwhelming. Even the smallest of things, such as getting up and going for food, was difficult. I made sure nobody knew because I always smiled.

Teresa: What was going through your head the moments before you took your own life?

Michelle: I was nervous and upset, not sure if I could go through with it, but I had to. There was no turning back. I could not complete my classes, and I had nowhere to turn.

So I ran up the stairs to the roof of the building, hoping that I would be tired. When I got up there, I got even more nervous, and I started breathing really heavy. Then I stopped and said to myself, "It is all going to be over." I ran and jumped.

Teresa: What happened next?

Michelle: I woke up without a body, but I could see everything, but not through my eyes. Everything felt nice and warm. I was happy.

There was an intense bright light all around me. It was so bright that the best way I can describe it, is to say that you'd think it would have blinded me, but it was inviting and loving. I didn't need to stand up, but I was standing up. I felt like I was home, but I was not at my house. There were so many feelings and sensations that I should not have understood, but I did. Everything was happening at once, but nothing was happening at all. I really cannot explain it using words. It is a feeling that we all live in.

I am told by the **ANGELS** that this is **HEAVEN.**

To use human words to describe something that I have never felt before is difficult. I am told by the **ANGELS** to tell you it is unconditional **LOVE,** and it feels like beautiful roses blooming freely in a meadow on a breezy, bright sunny day, while at the same time joyous music is playing over the mountaintops. I am free to run through the meadows filled with different colored wildflowers. I can do whatever I want. This is all being communicated to me as a knowing. I feel peaceful and joyous always.

At the same time there were many other spiritual beings there to greet me, each one having a different purpose. There was an **ANGEL** to help me adjust to my surroundings, showing me how to be without a body.

Michelle: There were many **ANGELS OF RESCUE** that help clean my energy field and remove the film and layers from the Earth.

I was told that I would have to go to the **HEALING HOSPITAL** so that they could work on me to help me adjust to living in **HEAVEN,** but before I went to the hospital, I got to meet and spend time with my **GUARDIAN ANGEL** (that I didn't know I had), my Grandparents and Boomer.

We had a celebration, and they told me that we were celebrating my arrival into **HEAVEN,** and that this was my birthday!! It was so joyous! I have never felt that free. In the Healing Hospital I spent a lot of time talking with my **ANGELS.**

Friends and family stopped by constantly to talk and teach me about my new life. Boomer was with me all the time. As I got stronger in my **SPIRIT,** my **GUARDIAN ANGEL** and a new group of **ANGELS** came to me and told me that I would not be hanging around there because there was work to be done. I asked them what they meant. I am in **HEAVEN,** and I can be free to be peaceful.

They proceeded to explain that since I took my own life I had to complete my **LIFE CONTRACT.**

I asked them, "What is a **LIFE CONTRACT?**" and they responded that it is a master blueprint of your life from the time you were born until the time you naturally die.

Michelle: I explained that I was already in HEAVEN, and that as far as I was concerned, my earthly life and the misery was over. They said, "We need to show you so you can understand."

They handed be a book that beamed with **LIGHT.** The **GOLDEN BOOK** had many names in different languages. All the names looked unfamiliar, but somehow I knew they were mine. They said, "You are correct. This is your book. The names are not important because the **LIGHT** that emanates from your book is your **LIGHT.** Each **SPIRITUAL** being has a unique **LIGHT** and that is how we are associated here in the upper realms of **HEAVEN.** No names are needed.

However, since you have not come to us naturally, we have exposed your name so we can show you your book."

I wanted to open the book from the first page. The book was pre-opened to my last day on earth. They said turn the page, and on the next page was information, and every page after that contained even more information. The book contained thousands of pages. I was not allowed to look at any of the details. They took the book away from me and asked, "Do you understand?" I nodded that I did.

Michelle leaves for the night. She returns several nights later to talk.

Teresa: Why are you alone?

Michelle: I want to talk to you privately.

Teresa: How are you doing?

Michelle: This is hard.

Teresa: What is hard?

Michelle: I have to work at making things work for the people still on Earth. I have to work with a team of other **SPIRITS** to make things right for the living. I did not think that this is what I would be doing!

Teresa: What did you think you would be doing?

Michelle: I thought I would be in **HEAVEN** and rest, hang out, do nothing. There are other **SPIRITS** here who do just that and have fun.

Not me! I am busy all the time, and to make matters worse, I got to see some of the future pages from my book. I did not like what I saw.

Teresa: What did you see?

Michelle: I was supposed to write articles about females in sports in other countries that would have inspired many women. My articles would have exposed political and financial corruption in certain countries that would have opened the doorway for females to succeed. In doing so, I was shown that my articles would have changed the life of two women. Now, the articles will never be written, and these two women will not have the information they need. There is more information that I have not seen. That was all I was shown.

Michelle paused for a long time. I remained quiet, and then she said:

Michelle: Have you read my book?

Teresa (taking a deep breath): Your book, as well as everybody else's book, is housed in the Library where all the books reside, including the Akashic Records. In order to read your book, I would have to be granted permission. Why do you ask?

Michelle: I know there was much more to my life, and I want to know more. I want to know if I was going to have a family. Was I going to get married? What was going to happen if I stayed on Earth?

Teresa: It is not up to me to give you what you ask for. You need to talk to your **GUARDIAN ANGEL.**

Michelle: When we were talking the other night, my **GUARDIAN ANGEL** whispered something in your ear, and I want to know what she said.

Right there I ask my **"TAG TEAM"** for help, and their response is that she will be exposed to the rest of her **CONTRACT** when she is ready.

Michelle overhears their response and she leaves.

When we pass into the **HEAVENS** and do our **LIFE REVIEW,** it is up to our **GUARDIAN ANGEL** and **"TAG TEAM"** to show us our **LIFE REVIEW.**

Sometimes our **LIFE REVIEW** can be very difficult to understand. That is why our review tends to occur in stages and take as long as needed. Not everyone who passes over does a **LIFE REVIEW.**

Suicides, from my experience, always do a **LIFE REVIEW.** Their agony and pain is an earthly experience.

When they are released from that turmoil and reside in **HEAVEN,** the love overtakes their **SPIRIT,** and they are renewed. This leaves them to be schooled in the next process of their work, including them wanting to look into their **CONTRACT** to see what remains. Everyone that I have interviewed says that there is an "awe moment", where they are taken aback by the information.

I am left feeling discouraged, and I question this whole process. I talk further with my **"TAG TEAM"** and question them about the viability of proceeding.

They tell me there are so many **SPIRITS** waiting to talk and tell me their stories, that I need to stay focused.

I ask them to show me (being the skeptical person that I am) that there are many **SPIRITS** that actually want their story told for the whole world to read.

In a momentary flash, the room fills up and the temperature is so hot that I can barely stand it.

I start to sweat (those of you who have not been to my Open Forum Public Events should know that when I work, it gets so hot for me that I keep the room freezing during the event because there are so many **SPIRITS** around), and I am overcome with sadness and grief.

Taking it all in, that there are so many adolescents that have committed suicide, overwhelms me. I ask them to take a step back until I can regain my composure.

It takes me a while to catch my breath and digest what I have just witnessed.

I ask my **"TAG TEAM"** how I am going to talk to everybody – there are so many adolescent **SPIRITS!!!**

They said that they would categorize them by their reason for committing suicide, knowing that each circumstance will be slightly different, as there are a lot of similarities in each of their stories.

I shake my head, as usual, being unsure, but I agree.

For the rest of the night, I walked the house talking to my kids, (my dogs, Halo and Wizard). I needed time to process the magnitude of what I saw. It would take me a few days to get a handle on my emotions and settle down before we could move forward.

CHAPTER SIX
OUT OF THE CLOSET AND THROUGH THE VEIL

*T*he sun is peeking through the vertical blinds in my bedroom, and it is way too early. I pull the covers over my head trying to go back to sleep, but I keep hearing the blinds move. I think to myself, "Why would the blinds be moving? The window is closed and the central air is on??!! It is just my imagination, I need more sleep."

This was one of the first nights in a long time that I was going to get to sleep through the night, so I roll over and try to fall back asleep, but the blinds are now even more open, and more light is shining in the room. I throw the covers off and get up to shut them, only to see a boy playing with the blinds.

Teresa: REALLY?? You're really in my bedroom? It is off limits!!

He shrugs his shoulders, and I kick him out of the room. I call for my **GUARDIAN ANGEL** and my **"TAG TEAM,"** and by this time I am really annoyed. My teacher shows up and tells me it is time to start again with more interviews. I tell her this is unacceptable! I need more sleep. I am tired. She agrees, and I go back to bed.

During the next day, I make a verbal proclamation that anyone who is hanging around, needs to follow the rules. Almost immediately, the same boy who had been messing with my bedroom blinds steps forward and apologizes.

A few nights later, Michelle arrives at 2:22 am with a group of **SPIRITS,** including the same boy that was in my room playing with the blinds.

I have not seen Michelle since that awkward night. As I approach her to talk, she interrupts me:

Michelle (very sternly): I am working.

Michelle's energy is different, and it makes me feel uncomfortable.

Michelle: This boy, his name is Dan, is impatient and wants to talk with you.

I have my recorder ready and ask him to follow me into my Reading Room where I conduct all the readings. As soon as we walk into the room he starts talking.

Dan: You do not need to ask me any questions. I saw you talk with Michelle, and I want to tell you my whole story. I was different. I like boys, and my father beat me for it. That is why I killed myself.

I am stunned. No one has ever started out that way. I have to stop him. I tried several times to stop him, but he keeps talking and showing me pictures. I ask my **"TAG TEAM"** to intervene. My team tries, he is full of conviction.

Teresa: Dan, slow down. You are sending the information quicker than I can understand.

Dan: Oh no. I want the world to know my/our story and look at all my friends here with me. They all have similar stories.

Teresa: Shut Up! I need a moment to absorb everything you just explained, and I need to record the information. Start again, but talk slower.

Dan: I could not take the beatings anymore from my father. I knew I was different from an early age and so did my father. My father was well respected in town and was active in the community and church.

70

My father was a businessman doing insurance and knew a lot of people. He wanted me to be just like his other sons, and he forced me to participate in sports. I didn't like football or baseball – and I wasn't good at any of them - but that did not stop my father from forcing me to play. My father would beat me on a regular basis because I was not playing well. My father would constantly compare me to my brothers and ask me why I couldn't be like them. My brothers were good athletes, and they were captains of their teams. They did okay in school, and I did great! I loved learning new things! I was really good at math and music, and I got A's and only two B's, where my brothers got C's and mostly D's.

My Dad never focused on the grades, only how well we did in sports, so he could brag about it to everybody.

He would tell me how my playing reflected poorly on him being a Dad. That is what I heard my entire life, "What is wrong with you? Why can't you catch the ball?" He would spend hours having me practice throwing and catching the balls. I never got better, and that infuriated him. He took it as if I was doing it on purpose, just to spite him for making me practice.

He would constantly berate me, telling me I was never going to be anything - which I knew, anyway. I was never going to be good enough. I was a thin, lanky boy who had long fingers and loved to play the piano. I could hear a song one time and be able to play it on the piano. Our next-door neighbor was a retired music teacher, and I would sneak over to her house, where she would let me play the piano in her living room. She would always tell me, "There is a life outside of this town. If you forget anything I have ever told you, remember there is more to life. Go find it." It always struck me as odd that she repeated this to me every time she saw me. She even wrote it down for me and would give me notes with the same saying, which I included in my poetry.

I loved spending time with her because she made me feel alive. She would put the radio on and taught me how to sing and dance. She had a beautiful voice. It would drive my father crazy when I would sing along with the radio. He took my radio away from me, and we were not allowed to have music in the house and definitely not in the car.

Going to games was torture for me. He would lecture me the entire time about how I needed to play better and what to do. This was my whole life. My father was focused on having great athletic sons just like he was when he was our age. He never cared about what we wanted or liked! When I asked for a guitar for Christmas he would respond, "What are you going to do with that?" Instead, I got more sports equipment. For my birthday one year, I asked for music lessons and sheet music. I got a rifle.

Teresa: Where was your mother?

Dan: Oh, she was there. She tried to stop him, but he dismissed her and told her to stay out of it. This was his son, and he would take care of it. My Mom was not a strong woman. She did what he told her. Privately, and on rare occasions, she would come and give me dinner in my room and try to comfort me when he was sleeping.

The kids in school and in the neighborhood would harass me about not being good at sports. Football was a big deal in our town in Texas. The neighborhood kids would always make fun of me. They would throw me down to the ground and tell me that I fight like a girl.

They would tease me about the way I would talk with my hands and the way I walked. They would tease me about everything, and I would come home and cry. One time they took my notebook away from me and read my poetry out loud, and everybody laughed. Another time they took a Polaroid of me dancing behind the bleachers and passed it all around school. That picture was talked about for months. I felt humiliated.

My father locked me in my room for weeks. When he would see me, he would either scream at me or slap me, and ask me how I could do this to him and the family.

They knew I was different. I knew I was different. But I did not know what that meant until I was an older teenager. I liked girls, but I liked boys much more. I kissed a girl once, but I had a crush on one of the guys on the football team. It lasted all through high school.

Nothing happened until after graduation when I started working at the gas station off the highway. I met a man that was not from around our parts. He was a salesman selling machine parts. He frequently drove through town in his brown Ford Bronco, and we'd get to talking. We found we had a lot in common. At first we were friends. He was the first person who I could talk about the things I liked. He was educated and did a lot of traveling, so he knew about a lot of things.

He would tell me that there is so much living outside of Texas. He told me stories about New York City and the Broadway plays he had seen. We got very close.

He was my first male kiss, and I was over the moon with happiness! We became closer and more than friends. I was happy! This went on for several weeks until a neighbor spotted me kissing him goodbye at the motel. She told my father that she was driving by and saw me at the motel kissing an older man (The nosy neighbor was having an affair herself!!)

When I got home, he started tossing the furniture around like it was cardboard, screaming and yelling that I had disgraced him and this family. He attempted to beat me but I got out of the house and ran back to the motel. There, my lover is packing to leave, and I tell him that I have run away from home and now we can be together. He looks very upset at this.

I ask him, "I thought this would make you happy. "He raises his left hand, and on his ring finger is a wedding band. He tells me he already has a wife, and she is pregnant with their second child.

I collapse, crying.

He tries to comfort me and tells me that he really cares for me, but that this was never meant to be a long-term thing. He said that he did not want me to find out this way. He did not want to hurt me. He tells me he was not going to say anything about his 'other life,' and that he was just going to leave about a week or so before I went off to college and not come back. "I am sorry I never meant for this to happen this way," he said, "I do care for you, and I want only the best for you."

I am so confused and destroyed. I am crying uncontrollably. He stayed for a while until I calmed down. He tells me to go to college and not look back. He kisses me goodbye and tells me again how sorry he is. He says he needs to get home and that I should stay at the motel for a couple of days until things cool off with my Dad back at home. He gives me money and leaves me alone at the hotel.

I do not remember how long I sat in that motel room before I was able to get myself together. When I finally did, it was dark outside. I left the motel and walked back home where I found my mother in the kitchen, weeping. I came in quietly, and when she saw me, she sprung up and threw her arms around me, crying even harder. She asked me if I was all right and where had I been the last two days. I just hugged her back and asked if there was anything to eat, realizing I had not eaten in two days. She took out some meat and made me a sandwich. I ate that one, in silence, and started another before I asked, "Where is he?" She said he was sleeping. It was well past midnight.

She told me to go off quietly to my room and get some sleep. When your father goes to work in the morning we will have time to talk. I did not want to talk. I did not want to deal with him or the family. I did not want to live. I had nothing to live for. I did not want to get beaten again. I did not want to say I was sorry, anymore. I did not want to talk. What was there to say? I did not want to talk to anyone.

Dan goes quiet for several minutes, and I am exhausted. Listening and watching his life was draining and upsetting.

Teresa: Can we talk later?

My "TAG TEAM" tells me go to bed to get needed rest. The amount of energy this takes out of me makes me feel like I am drunk.

I stagger to bed and sleep through the rest of the night and almost all the next day. When I finally wake up, I get out of bed and get ready

74

to feed and walk my dogs. That's when I see everybody waiting in the dining room.

My **"TAG TEAM"** tells me to go back to bed and get some more sleep, and that they do not want to leave, but they will not disturb me. Off to bed I go until early that night. I hear music as I am half asleep, and I know that **SPIRITS** are waiting. Still exhausted, I get out of bed and walk down the hall into my dining room, where Dan is entertaining everybody with his music. They all seem to be enjoying themselves.

I stay to listen and watch, and I start to feel better. Dan is dancing with Michelle and they are both laughing. There are so many adolescent **SPIRITS** in the room that I feel the need to turn to my **"TAG TEAM."**

Teresa: Why so many **SPIRITS?**

Their response blows me away.

"TAG TEAM:" These **SPIRITS** here have very similar stories and want to talk with you. What you do not see are the hundreds more who are observing and do not want to participate.

The energy in the room is filled with joy and happiness. I get myself something to eat, and my "TAG TEAM" joins me.

Teresa: This is taking a lot more out of me than I thought.

"TAG TEAM:" We agree. We will leave you alone for a while. You let us know when you want to start again.

Teresa: Thank you.

I finish my food, play with my dogs for a while and go back to bed to sleep the rest of the weekend.

Days go by, and I am now reading clients and not writing. It is too much for me to do both. The emotional, psychological and physical energy that each reading requires takes a little piece of me away.

I love the work that I do, helping people heal, helping them find closure and improving the quality of their life.

At the end of a long day, as I am closing my energy field, Dan, with Michelle by his side, pops into my reading room.

Dan: When are we going to talk again?

Teresa: Over the weekend.

This means nothing to him since there is no time on the other side , which sometimes I forget.

Teresa: I will call for you through my **"TAG TEAM."**

I tell my **"TAG TEAM"** that tonight will be a good night to start again. I fall asleep earlier than usual. Saturdays are always busy days. I am woken up at 2:22 a.m. with music. I know it is Dan, so I get up and walk into my Reading Room, and there he is with everybody else waiting. I say "Hi" to everybody, and I feel happy energy filling the room.

Dan: I want you to know that I am sorry about the last time. I did not realize you felt the pain and discomfort I was in as I was showing you my life. I will try not to be so vigorous when talking with you.

Teresa: Thank you. That would help.

Dan: The next several days after I came back home are quiet. I avoid everybody. I am not even sure Dad knows that I am home, because the boys (my brothers) are in the playoffs for the summer league. He is busy with them, and I stay in my room writing, crying and sleeping. I quit work. I know that my lover will not be back. I have no energy, and I do not want to do anything.

Mom comes in often to check on me, and I pretend to sleep when I am not actually sleeping. I do not want to talk. She leaves me notes about getting things ready to go off to college and how proud she is that I am the only son going off to get educated.

When nobody is home I go into the gun cabinet and take out the revolver. Dad had a stash of guns. A few more days go by, and it is my father's birthday.

I finish my letters that night. I put the gun to my head and pull the trigger.

There is silence in the room. I need to take a break.

I go make a cup of coffee to compose myself. I come back and there is still silence. I will never get used to doing this work.

There are so many questions I have. Before I could ask, Dan speaks.

Dan: I am ok now. I am no longer in pain.

Teresa: Can I ask you some questions?

Dan (with a smile): Sure

Teresa: I am not sure where to start, so let me just ask, "Why did you do it?"

Dan: I told you before that I did not want to get beaten anymore, and that there was nothing left to live for.

Teresa: You had college in a few weeks...

Dan: I was not going to college after what I went through in high school. College would be no different.

Teresa: Yes, it could've been different. You were going away from home, and you would have made new friends, and had a fresh new start!

Dan: No, it was going to be the same.

Teresa: Why on your Dad's birthday?

Dan: What better present to give him than me not being here! He would not have to be ashamed and embarrassed anymore. He no longer has to make excuses about me to his friends. He would no longer be angry.

Teresa: What about your Mom?

Dan: She would no longer have to hear him complain about me. He would stop abusing her.

Teresa: What was in the letters you wrote?

Dan: To sum it up briefly, I wrote to Dad and told him that I was not the son he wanted. I did not make him proud. I wrote that I tried to be the son he wanted. I worked really hard, but I was never going to be an athlete. I told him, "Despite everything, I love you."

To my Mom, to sum it up briefly, I wrote, "It is not your fault, it was mine. I love you, and I will miss you."

Teresa: Dan, can you relate to me anything unusual that happened to you before you passed?

Dan: What do you mean?

Teresa: Was there anything that got in your way that might have tried to stop you from committing suicide? Anything unusual?

There is silence.

Dan: I kept finding notes from Edith (the music neighbor) that I thought I had thrown away. In those notes, she had been telling me that there was more to life, and that I needed to go out and find it. While I was in my room, I kept hearing music, but I dismissed it. I thought I was hallucinating. There was no possible way there could be music in the house.

One day, when nobody was home, the doorbell rang. I got up to answer it, and when I opened the door there was nobody there. What I did find was a college pamphlet, tucked in front of the door. It wasn't from my college, where I was planning to attend but from a local college, and it said, "Come to college for a new experience."

Is that what you meant?

Teresa: Yes. Did you not think that was odd?

Dan: I was not paying attention. I was in pain. I hated my life.

Teresa: I am sorry for all that you went through. Is there anything that you would have changed about you committing suicide?

Dan: Since I have been in HEAVEN, I have met many SPIRITS. This is my friend Richard. He committed suicide the same way as me because he was gay. He has been here a shorter time than me.

Teresa: Hi Richard.

Richard: I also had a similar life, but my father did not beat me. My father ignored me as if I did not exist. I had exactly the same issues with my peer group.

Teresa: I am sorry.

Richard gives me a hug.

Dan steps in and introduces Juan.

Teresa: Hi Juan.

Juan: I had no father, and my mother had so many children that I felt left out. I liked feminine things. I loved wearing colors, feathers, big beads. I sewed my own clothing. We had little money so I would take my sisters' shirts and cut them up to make clothing for myself.

People laughed and made fun of me, too. I had a boyfriend, and we loved each other. Just like Dan, I had no friends and nowhere to turn. I have been here a while, but not as long as Dan. After my boyfriend killed himself with drugs, I hung myself.

He smiles and his lover, Fernando, steps forward. They are holding hands.

At that moment I got the chills. They both hug me and tell me to keep writing, as there are many more.

Dan steps forward with a very young handsome looking boy. He is wearing more modern clothing.

Young Handsome Boy: I took my own life with a gun. I could not take the abuse any longer from my church, my school and the neighbors. My parents loved me. They were great, and they knew I was gay even before I knew I was gay. They loved me and supported me no matter what! But I still felt as if I was never going to fit in, and no matter what was happening, my being gay was wrong.

Teresa: Who told you that?

Young Handsome Boy: We lived in a big church community. Neighbors, church elders and some of the kids in school all told me how wrong it was to be gay. There was no place for me.

Teresa: Were there any signs that you got from the **ANGELS** before you left?

Young handsome boy knew exactly what I meant due to his church background.

Young Handsome Boy: I often found little white feathers around me. They were on my shirt. One was even floating in the air the day I killed myself. I got a call from my grandmother, out of the blue, asking me to come visit her, and she lived in another state. She had never done that before.

Teresa: Thank you.

I give him a big hug and tell him he is always welcome in my home. He hugs me back and steps aside.

Next is another young man wearing a football uniform.

Football player: I tried to hide my attraction to boys. I dated girls so nobody would know. In college, no one knew my secret, not even my friends or family. I was considered the Casanova of the campus! I got great grades in school, and I had girls throwing themselves at me.

I came from a loving, happy family, the type of family that everybody admired. My parents supported us, ran around with us to games, practices and all our after-school activities. I had friends and got along with everybody. I hung around with all different groups while I was in high school. I got a football scholarship and played college football and did very well, until one night when I got drunk and got caught with another player in my dorm room.

My secret was out. I tried to downplay it, but it didn't work. All my teammates looked at me as if I had a disease and shunned me. I couldn't take it. My grades started to slip, and I sunk into a deep depression.

Like everybody else who has experienced these things, I felt as if there was no way out. One night I took a bunch of pills and drank a bottle of vodka. And here I am talking with you.

Teresa: You are smart. You knew there was help. Why did you not get help?

Football player: I went to the college help line. They did not help. They could not take away the looks and ribbing from my teammates. They could not take away my new reputation as being the gay Casanova. It became the big joke on campus. I could not take it anymore. I broke down. The only way out for me was suicide.

My reputation was everything! How and what everybody thought of me, my reputation was the most important thing to me!! How do you change that once the cat is out of the bag?

Teresa: Did anything unusual happen before you passed?

Football player: I kept running into my old coaches in the weeks before.

Football player: They would regale me with old memories of how well I did as a player, how many people still talk about me, saying that I was a success and a role model for other kids to do well and go to college on a scholarship. My pictures are still up in the high school trophy cabinet.

Dan gives him a hug and he steps back.

A tall, big boy steps forward and tells me his name is Joe.

Joe: I want to talk with you.

Teresa: You are welcome to talk with me.

Joe: Dan helped me cross over into **HEAVEN.** My story is similar to Dan's. All these young men have Dan to thank for helping them into **HEAVEN.**

Joe is so polite as he speaks with me. He tells me that his story is slightly different in one respect: his father was a biker. He loved to ride Harleys and loved his son. When he came out to his dad, his father did not handle it very well. His dad did not know how to talk with Joe after that revealing conversation, and he simply stopped talking with his son. Joe tells me that his dad took the news very poorly, and since he and his father had been so close, it was like a death to him.

Joe and his father did everything together. Joe said that he started drinking, and on his twenty-first birthday he got really drunk. In his grief he took a gun, put it in his mouth and pulled the trigger.

Joe: I was so full of loneliness and grief that I was not thinking. I was distraught over my father's rejection. There was nothing anybody could do to change the events. My dad is a stubborn, proud man who could not handle having a gay son.

Teresa: I am sorry for your grief.

Joe: Ma'am, you are welcome. I am glad to be here to tell my story.

Teresa: Was there anything that happened that was unusual before you passed?

Joe: Yes ma'am, I kept hearing my mother's name. Different women at the bar would introduce themselves to me every night, and one of them was named Virginia. I would smell her perfume often and know she was around.

I found her funeral card the day before I passed. It just fell out of my wallet. I did not even know I had it. My mom had passed from cancer when I was very young, and her final words to me were, "Son I love you. You are the best thing I ever did. I do not want you to cry. I want you to remember me being happy, loving you. I want you to live long and happy."

Teresa: What did you think when you kept having this happen?

Joe: I knew she was around. I just kept drinking. I was filled with anger, fear and grief. I needed to forget. I was lost in my own despair.

Teresa: How are you now?

Joe: When I saw the **LIGHT** I was embraced by my mother's love. She wrapped her arms around me and held me like she did when I was a child. My mother's appearance is the same as I remember her with a vibrant smile and her deep blue eyes filled with joy. She is happy and healthy here in **HEAVEN.**

Her love, with the assistance of the **HEAVENLY REALM,** has allowed me to heal. I am at peace fulfilling my obligations. I regularly leave dimes for my dad as signs that I am sending him love.

Teresa: Is there anything else you would like to tell me?

Joe: Arriving into **HEAVEN** the way that I did does not allow me to stay with my Mom. I missed her my whole life, and if I had not taken my life we could be together enjoying the heavenly world. I will forever work to ensure that my contract's commitment is fulfilled. Therefore, I will be attached to the earth while my Mom lives in a higher heavenly realm.

Teresa: What do you mean?

Joe: Within the heavenly world are different levels of **LIGHT** and **LOVE.** Those of us who take our own lives have to live in **HEAVEN** connected to the Earth. Those who do not take their own lives get to ascend to a higher heavenly life. Living in that life is much different than the life I lead. I will not be able to ascend into that beautiful life. If I knew what I knew now I would have stayed and finished out my earthly life.

Teresa: Thank you for sharing your story.

Joe steps back.

A young woman steps into my view and she smells like sweet honeydew. She looks like a dancer.

Dancer: I always liked playing with dolls and play dress up. I loved putting mom's makeup on and would always wear her clothing when I was a little girl. I loved looking beautiful. My mom put me in beauty pageants and I won many, many trophies.

As I grew up, boys were always hanging around me. As I got older, I was asked out a lot. I did go on dates, if you want to call them that. We went for pizza or hung out at the ice cream shop or went to a movie. One or two of them kissed me, and I found it awkward. They would even try to feel me up, and I just felt nothing. I pushed them away. I did not know why, but I found other girls more fascinating and wanted to spend time with them. I had a steady boyfriend in my senior year of high school. He was my first. It was nothing special. We "did it" a lot because he wanted to. It was all right.

I went to college on a scholarship for dance, and I loved being with girls. One day after dance, another dancer from another college was there for a competition. Our eyes met, and I felt something. She did, too. We called each other a lot and in our conversations we learned we lived only 30 minutes away from each other's hometown. During break, we met and hung out, and that was my first time with a woman. She had been with other woman before me. I was in bliss. I wanted to spend all my time with her. I even tried to transfer to her college but my scholarship would not allow it. We decided to see other people, which was fine with me. I was happy to explore. During my freshman year in college, I was happy to find myself! But in my sophomore year, it got hard. I met a college professor who took an interest in me, and I found it mentally stimulating. We got intimate quickly, and I found myself being interested in him. We were involved for a while, but he broke it off when he said it was getting "too serious." I found myself feeling confused and even in a funk. I was not interested in anybody for a while after that. The pressure from school was becoming more difficult, and I was involved in many things.

I met a woman who I thought was my soul mate, and we fell in love. We ended up having a topsy-turvy relationship that screwed with my head. One moment we were good together, the next we were arguing. She was angry and confused and would tell me it was my fault that things are like this. My hair started falling out, and my dance was off. My grades were slipping. I started self-medicating for anxiety, and it turned into a drug addiction.

I did not know how to handle the pressure, and I was not thinking clearly. I felt like everything, including my looks, was slipping away. I stopped dancing. All I wanted was my next fix and so did my partner. I started sleeping with men and women, all for money. One day I looked in the mirror and saw someone I did not recognize and who I did not like. I had enough.

I did too much cocaine on purpose. I had enough.

*Dan and several other **SPIRITS** step forward to tell me their stories, which are extremely similar. My **"TAG TEAM"** shows me there are hundreds of **SPIRITS** in **HEAVEN** watching us talk. They too have gotten to **HEAVEN*** *this way.*

These conversations are over several nights and on the very last night.......

DAN: You asked me several nights ago if there was anything that I would have changed about my committing suicide. My answer is that all of these adolescents who you have spoken with would not have committed suicide if I had lived and been there on earth. I was supposed to go to college and through my personality, my love of music and the arts, I would have helped these people and together we all would still be living.

I would have started an underground support group where we would have all met. Through that and through similar interests and introductions, we would all have overcome and lived.

I was supposed to work at the college as my first job and be there for several years implementing the Arts Program. All these **SPIRITS** would have lived out their **LIFE CONTRACTS** as well, and there would have been magnificent things that these young people would have done and achieved!

Joe would have worked with his dad, and they would have designed a new type of safer motorcycle.

Juan and Fernando would have had their clothing business, designing costumes for shows.

Michael (the young handsome boy) would have lead a movement for gays that would have helped change the view of his community, thereby saving even more lives, himself.

Brad (the football player) would have gone on to be a professional football player and start a children sports program for troubled kids, and his foundation would have built a homeless shelter.

Amy (the dancer) would have gotten help, and she would have gone on to work at the United Nations to start a dance program for girls in third world countries. She would have had two children of her own, and they would have had children, and so on. A whole family line gone!

None of this will happen, not now or ever! I destroyed my life, and in doing so, I destroyed so many others by not being alive. This, I will have to rectify until my **LIFE CONTRACT** is up. Then and only then, will I be able to live in **SPIRIT** peacefully. But there will forever be damage that I have done to the universe by removing myself too early.

If I would have had more help and knowledge that things would have gotten better, I might have stayed on Earth. If I understood that there was truly more to life and that I had responsibilities to other people, it might have been different.

If I had understood that there really are **ANGELS** and **SPIRITS** helping me, I know I would have found more comfort.

That is why we all want you to tell our stories. There is so much more to life, and there is help for others who experience what we were going through in those times. There is help. There is a **FUTURE**.

There were consequences, that while living on earth, we were not aware of, and now we want other adolescents to know that we are helping.

Having difficult times and grief and brokenness, does not mean that life is over. These are just bumps in the road, obstacles to be overcome and made stepping stones into a long successful life.

CHAPTER SEVEN
IT'S NOT YOUR FAULT

1 fell asleep on the sofa with my cell phone, and the TV blaring woke me up. I look around the room, and it's filled with Michelle's friends. They're back for another night of conversation.

Michelle: We have to talk.

I can see that she is in a good place, for her energy is different than the last several times we had spoken - that professional demeanor is not there, and she looks more comfortable, happy and relaxed.

I welcome everybody into my home.

Teresa: Michelle, what would you like to talk about?

Michelle: There are many people here who want to talk to you. You and I will talk privately later. We've all decided that Wendy is going to tell her story because it represents many other adolescent suicides that are here right now in this room.

Michelle brings forth Wendy. She is a slender, slightly tall young woman. She looks to be about in her late teens to early 20s, long brunette hair, fit and has a gentle soul.

Wendy: Hi. I'm Wendy and I am 19 years old.

I can tell that Wendy is from the Midwest area, and she has been on the other side for a couple of years.

I immediately notice that Wendy is very logical and thinks in a pragmatic way. I do not feel any emotions from her. She is a little too reserved.

Teresa: How do you want to do our interview tonight?

Wendy: I have seen so many interviews that you have done with the other **SPIRITS,** so I am just going to tell my story. You can ask me questions as I tell my story.

Teresa: Ok.

Wendy: I am a very bright, successful woman who wanted to be a lawyer. I did extremely well in school. I was ahead of my class. I took many AP courses in high school, so when I went to college I was on the fast track. I wanted to change the world. I wanted to stand up for women's rights, family issues and children of neglect and abuse. .

I come from a divorced family. My father was a narcissist, a perpetual liar and manipulator. He was very abusive and argumentative. He enjoyed controlling every situation.

My mother stayed with him for several years, and it took such a toll on her. I saw my mother become a shadow of herself. I tried to get Mom to go with me to counseling, but she refused.

I was the oldest and had two younger brothers. There is a significant age gap between them and me. I was determined to never be like my mother. I wanted to be educated and successful. I worked very hard in school to be a straight A student. I was a cheerleader, played softball and was co-captain of the team for two years. I also loved acting, and I was in some school plays. I was very good at chess, and I was the captain of my debate team for 3 years.

All of my life I've tried to help everyone. I tried to save my mother from my father, and it wasn't until my teenage years that I realized, through my friendship with my debate teacher, that I couldn't save her.

My teacher said I needed to save myself, so through her help, I got counseling. I realized I was basically on my own from an early age, and even though my mother and father said they loved me, they were too busy with their own issues to really get to know me.

I had friends. I socialized. Life was very good for me. I have never really had to struggle with anything. Everything else came easy. I never wanted for anything or needed to work for anything because my parents were financially comfortable. Life was good growing up. I had every convenience possible - new computers, phones, anything that was new, I had it. I didn't know what it was like not to have what I asked for.

Teresa: Sounds like you had a wonderful life.

Wendy: I absolutely did.

Teresa: How was the communication between you and your parents when you were younger?

Wendy: We would talk on the phone. On the weekends we would all sit down and catch up about the week.

Teresa: How often did your family get together for food, fun or just hang out?

Wendy: Most of the time I was at practice, a game or an event, so I saw my parents when I got home in the evening. We would have casual conversations. They would ask me about my day, I would respond and then go to my room.

Teresa: Who drove you to all your school events?

Wendy: Most of the time they started right after school so I stayed at school until I was done. Then, either Mom or Dad would pick me up. If not, I would get a ride with a friend, and they would drop me off home.

Teresa: When did you do your homework and eat?

Wendy: "Most of the time I did my homework in study class or between classes. It was easy, and I ate when I got home. There was food in the refrigerator, and I would warm it up.

Teresa: Did your parents put pressure on you to succeed?

Wendy: "They never said anything. I would hear them talk about me, and they were proud, but would never encourage me either way. When I was in high school, I was always at the top of my class. I graduated at the top of my class magna cum laude and had received several scholarships for college. My performance in softball and my grades gave me the scholarships to college even though my parents would have had no problem paying for college. It was so easy in high school. I didn't have to really study in high school.

College was so different. The volume of work and playing softball consumed all my time. I had to work hard all the time to stay on top to get good grades. I felt like it was never ending. My advisor in college suggested that I get a tutor to help me learn how to study. I did, and it really did help.

Teresa: How many credits did you take your first year?

Wendy: Sixteen.

Teresa: Why so many credits and softball?

Wendy: I thought I could handle it. High school was easy. I had no idea college was so overwhelming. Every day I struggled to be on top. I thrived on the competition. It was hard, but I did manage to be in the top 3%. I did not like not being number one. I was determined to do better next year.

During the summer I took more study courses and learned how to read faster. I felt stronger to handle the course load the second year.

Teresa: What about your social life? How was campus life that first year?

Wendy: I made some friends, and I also had my teammates from the softball team. My focus was on my grades.

Teresa: What did you do for fun?

Wendy: I went to a few parties, but I studied constantly.

Teresa: Did you join any clubs or pledge to any sororities?

Wendy: No. (I can tell that Wendy is getting a little frustrated with my questions)

Teresa: Wendy, what caused you to take your life?

Wendy: My sophomore year started out a little rough. I was still struggling, but once I got into the groove and utilized all that I learned in the study courses, I had more time to enjoy campus life. I started to socialize, and I started dating.

I fell in love with another college student, and it changed my life. I had not known what it felt like to be in love or loved in this way.

Josh was my first kiss. He held me in a way no one has ever held me before! He was deeply interested in my life. We shared many common interests including sports, the love of debating and the competition to be on top.

Teresa: Tell me about this relationship.

Wendy: We spent every day together studying and laughing. We had so much in common. He was my better half. I looked forward to being with him every day. We ate every meal together, hung out together. He even came to all my practices and games. We were inseparable.

Teresa: Was this your first relationship?

Wendy: Yes. He was the first person I ever dated. How magical it was that I found my true love on my first date! We talked about spending the rest of our lives together.

Teresa: How long were you together?

Wendy: We were together for about nine months.

Teresa: What happened?

Wendy: I found he had a girlfriend at home and that I was his college girlfriend. I was destroyed. My whole world fell apart. He wanted nothing to do with me. He said I was too clingy and that he loved me, but it could not work out. I asked him why, and he said it was over. I cried and kept trying to get him to come back, but he wanted nothing to do with me.

I couldn't understand what was going on. Why did he not want to be with me? This went on for days then weeks. During this time I went to classes and couldn't focus.

My grades starting slipping, and everything came crashing down around me. I was making mistakes in the field. We lost two games because of my errors. I missed paper deadlines, and I couldn't focus.

I felt like my life was over. I couldn't do it anymore. Why was I doing it? What was the point of it all? I kept asking that question all the time. In the middle of the semester, my advisor approached me and told me that my scholarships were in jeopardy, and in that moment, I realized that I was done.

I didn't have the energy or interest to work that hard to be on top. What was it all for? I kept playing that question over and over in my head for days. One night there was a party that my teammates took me to where everyone was having a good time, and I felt like I did not belong. I could not relate to what was going on, and I felt so detached and lost. Where was I? What was all of this about?

I knew then there was no need to continue. I had lost the love of my life, my grades were irreparable and I had been benched for the first time ever. I decided that night I was done. I came home, put the chair under the fan, threw a rope, tied a knot, stood on the chair and hung myself.

At this point the graphic image was so overwhelming for me, I needed to take a break. It would be many, many days before I could come back to talk with Wendy about her life.

I am in my kitchen making dinner, and I feel someone watching. I turn around and the room is filled with spirits, and Michelle touches my back.

Michelle: How are you doing?

Teresa: I am getting better. Interviewing so many **SPIRITS** and writing their life stories is more than I had bargained for. The psychological and emotional toll it has taken has affected every aspect of my life.

There are times I feel like I am in a whirlwind having trouble dealing with my own life, never mind all the other spirits. It is tough to do this work. When I am reading people, it is different.

I communicate with **SPIRITS** and deliver sensitive, emotionally charged information that pertains to their friends, family and themselves. The reading focuses on their lives and what has transpired in their life while they are still living.

In conducting these interviews, I spend hours talking with each **SPIRIT.** The information focuses more on their **LIFE CONTRACTS,** consequences and the impact that this will have on their family, friends and the world. While engaging in these interviews, the depth of information and emotions of the lives of these SPIRITS can sometimes have the effect of sucking the life right out of me.

I know this is what I signed up for, and I am glad to do it. I just never realized it would be so intense and life changing.

Michelle: We have been watching you and there have been many **HEALING ANGELS** around to help you rejuvenate your energy. You will need to rest and sleep for a while longer before we can continue.

Teresa: I agree. *(I notice that the room returns to the normal temperature.)*

The room fills with the smell of flowers, and the lights dim down. I know this is **SPIRIT'S** way of letting me know that they are here.

Michelle steps forward and has smile on her face.

Teresa: What's up?

Michelle: My mom will be calling you for another reading. I have been going to her and working with her, and it is time for her to talk with me. Are you ready for more work?

I nod.

Wendy steps forward beaming with loving light.

Wendy: I am ready to continue our interview.

Teresa: OK, let's talk about what happened before you committed suicide. Did you get help?

Wendy: No

Teresa: Why not? You had been in counseling before and you had success?

Wendy: No, I did not think about counseling. My heart was broken. How do you fix a broken heart by talking to a counselor? I wanted Josh back.

I can feel Wendy's frustration and pain over this line of questioning. Her tone with me is becoming more intense.

Teresa: Did anybody offer you help like friends or teammates?

Wendy: Yes, there were many people around me trying to encourage me to snap out of it. They tried to get me to go to get help from campus counselors. I wanted to talk to Josh. I needed to talk with him!!!!

Teresa: Did you commit suicide solely because of Josh breaking up with you?

Wendy: Mostly yes, but then everything else starting happening. I could not play ball. I felt like I had two left feet on the field. I didn't take notes in class and I did not keep up with the homework assignments. I struggled with everything.

As she answers my questions and I can feel her impatience and lack of emotional maturity.

Teresa: Did anything unusual happen before you took your life?

Wendy: You have asked that question to everybody you have talked with so far, and I can tell you no.

With that answer my **"TAG TEAM"** steps in to tell me that she did not notice the interactions from them.

They did send many messages to help her. At her last game she met up with her friend from high school on the opposing team who talked to her and said she was not looking well. The girl had given Wendy her number and told her to call to talk.

Wendy had found a scarf attached to a branch on her way to class that reminded her of her old debate teacher. The scarf smelled like her teachers signature perfume. That was a sign for Wendy to reach out and call her. Wendy did have her telephone number since they were still in contact. Wendy put the scarf in her bag. She had subsequently taken it out the night before to smell it. Then the phone rang, but she did not pick it up.

It was us trying to get her the message to call. There were many people who offered their help but she refused to let them in to help.

Wendy: All that I wanted to do was talk to Josh. I have not been allowed to see him since I am here nor will I go to him now. That is not allowed.

Teresa: How long have you been there?

Wendy: A long time.

Teresa: Over ten years?

Wendy nods.

Teresa: What have you learned since you have been in **HEAVEN?**

Wendy: I should not have taken my life. I had a long life ahead of me including a famous career, children, grandchildren and a true lover. I was supposed to write a bill for Congress on spousal and child abuse. It would have become law in my state. I would have been instrumental in woman's legal issues such as rape, domestic violence and divorce.

There is so much more to life than a grade, a game and a lover. I defined myself through all those things, and I now know I was much more than all of that. I was special. I had a mission and I was going to change the world.

What was happening to me at the time was just that, at the time. I now know that it would have passed, and there was something better waiting for me. I didn't know I had a future, and it was already waiting for me.

Wendy: As I live here in **SPIRIT,** I now have to orchestrate and fulfill my **LIFE CONTRACT** as an outsider.

With a full spiritual team, I have to make sure that the situations and experiences others were supposed to have while I was alive, still happen. Do you have any idea how difficult that is?

I am constantly working to make sure all the other **LIFE**

CONTRACTS that were connected to mine are executed. My work will go on for lifetimes!!

I will not be able to rest in peace. I will reside in **HEAVEN** but not enjoy all the glory and peace that **HEAVEN** allows.

There is silence in the room for a long time.

Michelle steps forward and tells me that this how everybody feels when they have had the opportunity to review their life. It is a complicated review involving so many people that the lessons are life altering. They also want to acknowledge it is not only their lives that have been affected, but they have also altered the lives of those they have left behind on Earth.

There is much sorrow because of the pain and suffering they have caused. So much healing work has to be done for both sides of the veil -- the living and the afterlife.

Michele and Wendy step forward and have so many SPIRITS with them that I feel this is going to be a long night.

Wendy: I have a special friend that I want you to meet. She is the representative of this large group of SPIRIT. They want to tell you why they committed suicide. Teresa, this is Cindy.

Cindy: Can you really talk to me?!

Teresa: Yes. I can talk to you, and I can also see you. You have red long, flowing hair, your body is slender and you have deep blue eyes.

Cindy (she starts to cry): YES, YES, YES!!!!!

I approach her and give her a hug, and she calms down.

Teresa: What would you like to tell me?

Cindy: I speak for all of the women here tonight. Their stories are extremely similar to Wendy's and Michele's except with one notable difference.

She starts to cry again.

Teresa: How can I help you?

Cindy: I have never ever spoken to anyone about what happened to me, and this is why everyone chose me to tell their stories.

Cindy hands me a remote and a screen appears.

Cindy: I want you to see what happened. I cannot tell you, but I can show you.

She proceeds to tell me the beginning of her story.

Cindy: Most of us went to college, and all of us were successful and smart. Some of us joined sororities, some of us joined clubs and some of us were activists. Most of us went to different colleges and had different interests and majors. Almost all of us were in shape and were athletic, participating in school functions. We all were happy women with fairly functional families and lives until we were raped. Each one of us was raped in a different way. Most were on college campuses, and most never got justice. For me, I never got to tell my story, so I was elected to tell my story.

At this point the screen lights up as it has done in the past, and the movie begins. I see her and this man walking side by side.

Teresa: A date?

Cindy: She nods.

Teresa: Did you know him?

Cindy: She nods.

Teresa: How did you know him? Was he in your classes?

Cindy: She nods.

I can see they seem to be enjoying each other's company. They are walking, and I can see they were at a party for a while. He looks like an average college guy. As I watch, nothing seems out of the ordinary. I can hear them talking about themselves. They are laughing.

The picture changes, and they are in a room. It looks like a guy's room.

Teresa: His room?

Cindy: She nods.

I continue to watch. It looks like a normal date. He leans over for a kiss. She accepts. They talk. Then he starts to get aggressive, and Cindy starts to cry.

*I can feel the love from the **SPIRITS** in the room surround her for support.*

I wait as she composes herself.

The images start up again, and he has cornered her on the couch.

I can see she is fighting back, and I can hear her tell him, "No, stop! Get off of me!" She continues to fight, yelling at him to stop. He ignores her and continues ripping off her panties and then having his way with her.

Cindy starts to cry again and then fights backs the tears so I can continue. We pause for a while. I need to regain some strength and courage to continue to watch.

The next image I see is Cindy getting up looking dazed and confused.

He has a smile on his face and looks like the cat that just ate the canary. Cindy gathers up her things running out of the room crying. There is blood running down her leg. She runs out of the building and the next scene is her room.

I turn to her, and she is still weeping. I tell her I am so sorry. I give her a hug, and we both cry.

I compose myself, taking a deep breath.

Teresa (to her "TAG TEAM"): Are we done?

"TAG TEAM:" There is a lot of work to be done.

The screen lights up again, and I see Cindy has a bottle of vodka and some pills. The next image is her funeral.

There are so many people at the wake. The line goes out the building and around the block.

Cindy: I never knew so many people cared and loved me.

My **"TAG TEAM"** shows me that Cindy was a loving caring person who helped anyone who needed help. She went out of her way to care for others. I see many people talking to her parents about how she helped them. I can see by the expressions on their faces that they did not know how many people she helped along the way. I can see the pride and love they have for her and how her passing has deeply hurt them.

Cindy: It was not my way to boast about what I did. I did it because it was the right thing to do. I am so upset that I have has caused so much pain. That was not my intent.

Teresa: Why did you not get help?

Cindy: I was ashamed, and I did not want anybody to know. I blame myself for letting this happen to me.

Teresa (giving her a big hug): I am so sorry that this happened to you.

I can feel her energy changing to a lighter, happier vibration.

She points behind her and I see hundreds of SPIRITS in the room that have been date raped and subsequently took their own lives.

There are many **SPIRITS** stepping forward talking about being date raped and brutalized during their attacks.

Stephanie, a young, warm spirit steps forward and tells me she represents a very large group of girls. She was the average college student enjoying college life until she was raped walking to her dorm from the library one night. He beat her first and then raped her.

That night changed her whole life. She was never the same, even with help and support. She could not continue to live with the images that flooded her every waking day and night. She took too many sleeping pills and woke up in the arms of her grandmother and her dog Trixie by her side.

She tells me that she is sorry. She should have stayed. She would have been the one to put her attacker away before he did this to many other women before he was killed.

There are so many diverse women here in the room with me. Some are dressed like hippies from the 60's, some have those beehive hair styles. Their styles are telling me that they represent different years in history. A woman named Jody represents a group of **SPIRITS** and she steps forward.

Jody: All of us were date raped and became pregnant from the rape. Our families did not believe in abortion and wanted us to have the babies.

I get my sign for PTSD (post-traumatic stress disorder) from my **"TAG TEAM."**

Jody: We could not do it.

Teresa: Could there have been anything done to change their actions?

A tall, beautiful woman with a southern accent steps forward. She tells me her name is Rachael.

Rachael: I come from a devoted, loving family whose beliefs are grounded in Christianity and so did many of the SPIRITS families. I speak for all the SPIRITS here. We were children put into an impossible position, faced with a life filled with shame and stigma that we were raped and that our potential child was the product of that rape.

Our families would not change their beliefs, and we had no place to turn. Abortion was not allowed. If we were able to have an abortion, many of us would have stayed and lived a full life.

I thank them for coming forward to tell their story.

Another group steps forward all talking very loudly. Mary introduces herself to me.

Mary: All of these women with me had a voice. They told authorities about their rape. I told the college, the Dean, the Residence Assistant, the Police and no one believed me!

She and all the women with her were raped by men who were either athletes in college or men who held authority positions within the community.

They were branded and shamed by the governing authorities. Some were told it was their fault by the way they dressed and their dating history. Others were told they should not have put themselves in that position.

Mary: Almost all of us were made to feel like we were not worth anything. What was the point - we were worthless! For most of us, it broke us and that is why we are all here tonight!

Taking our own lives, we now know was not the answer - it was a way out.

All of us now work hard to make sure that the **LIFE CONTRACTS** that we intentionally voided will be fulfilled.

Teresa: Mary, is there anything that could have been done to change their actions?

Mary: It is people's perceptions that need to change. All the **SPIRITS** here tonight were children and young adults who were innocent victims and never knew they were truly innocent.

My "TAG TEAM" tells me that every spirit has an individual rape story.

Each life has value. Each story is important. Every **SPIRIT** is celebrated for their bravery and courage. Gathered here tonight, they have grouped themselves together to help tell their story that shame, guilt and blame are the reasons why almost all of these women took their own lives.

If each of them would have lived out their **LIFE CONTRACT,** many of these women would have been instrumental in changing the way rape is perceived.

Some would have become early pioneers in implementing new policies and unifying rape data bases to catch their rapists.

Some would have helped other victims, and some would have become spokeswomen for different causes.

Some would have done their own investigations and been responsible for catching their rapists.

Wendy steps forward and tells me that there are SPIRITS here tonight that she would have met along the way in her life that she could have helped because she would have been influential in organizing a survivor's clinic that would have helped girls heal.

Since she was not there to help, others took her place but there is no substitute for an individual.

As I sit here tonight, I see all the **SPIRITS** holding hands in communion with each other. Their stories are similar. Their outcomes are the same.

In **SPIRIT,** the bonds that are formed through life tragedies connect these adolescents and will take lifetimes to correct and heal. They not only have to carry those spiritual wounds into eternal life, they will also have to work to heal them and help fulfill their **LIFE CONTRACTS** for those who are still on Earth.

Living in the light and love of **HEAVEN** make it all possible but never ending. There is no peace, only constant commitment to the others left behind.

The sadness and pain that fill my heart from each story will remain with me forever.

CHAPTER EIGHT
THINK OUTSIDE THE BOX

Knock, Knock.......... It's very dark in my bedroom, and I look around and notice that the power is out.

I look towards the door and there is Michele with my **"TAG TEAM"** and **SPIRITS** waving at me. I pull the covers over my head.

Teresa (thinking to myself): It has been weeks since I have worked on the book. I am still devastated and overwhelmed from the last interviews. I really do not want to continue.

"TAG TEAM:" You cannot hide under the covers forever.

Teresa: Go away! I am tired, and I do not want to do this anymore!

I close my eyes and fall back to sleep.

For a long time my **"TAG TEAM"** does not bring up the book until weeks later **when I am in the shower, and they ask, "ARE YOU READY?"**

Teresa: NO! I AM NOT!! I do not want to do this anymore! It is too draining!!

The water goes cold to get my attention, which, by the way, **they have always done to get my attention.**

"TAG TEAM" (shouting at me): YOU ARE THE ONLY ONE

WHO CAN DELIVER THIS INFORMATION, AND YOU KNOW WHY!!!!!!

Teresa: I don't care!! I am done!!

"TAG TEAM" (shouting louder): There are many SPIRITS counting on you to tell their stories!! There is a lot of work to be done to help people. It is time to start again. You are the only one who can deliver this book, and you know why.

This debate goes on for a few minutes in the cold shower. I try desperately to get the water to warm up, and I know that until I concede, I will be in the cold.

In my heart I know they are correct. Given the vast experience I have had working with both worlds, I am best equipped to deliver the messages that can potentially change the world. So I agree to start again in a few days. The water turns hot again, and I finish my shower.

My cell phone is ringing. It is 2:22 a.m. My cell phone is programmed not to ring from midnight until 10:00 a.m., but I know who it is, so I turn over and try to ignore the constant ringing. The ringing grows louder and louder, and I cannot fall back to sleep.

I get up, turn the phone off and get dressed. I walk down my hallway and everybody is waiting in the living room. My house is filled with more SPIRITS than I have ever had since the conception of writing the book.

My **"TAG TEAM"** greets me first, and I give a nod, then Michele greets me. I walk into the kitchen to make myself a cup of tea. I can hear everyone talking.

They are so excited to be in my house!! I walk into the living room.

Teresa: How are we going to proceed tonight?

"TAG TEAM:" Most of these people are here to observe and are part of the same group.

I can feel that the energy is mostly male.

Teresa: Why so many young men?

"TAG TEAM:" These young men are very special **SPIRITS.** They were part of the Indigo Children who had come to Earth. They had special gifts and could not adjust to life on Earth.

Teresa: You mean the young adults that are considered unique and special, such as folks who are autistic or have autistic spectrum disorder or the highly intelligent?

"TAG TEAM:" YES.

EVERY SPIRIT IN THE ROOM CLAPS

Michelle: Can George tell his story?

All the **"TAG TEAMS"** here in my living room know that George's story will resonate with many young people today.

Michelle helps George step forward.

Teresa: Hi, George.

George: I want you to put my story in the book for others like me. I do not tell my story to hurt my family in any way. My family is very important to me, and that is a very important part of our culture. I am a Japanese-American boy whose parents are very traditional.

They brought me up with very strict, very old traditions and values that were ingrained in them during their own upbringing. They told me to work hard, and they pushed me to strive for excellence as early as I can remember. My parents loved me and put a lot of time and energy into my upbringing. They focused on my education and my mind every day. I was very smart from a young age, doing mathematical problems and reading far above my age, long before I ever went to school. I won many awards for math and science.

As far back as I could remember, I would take things apart and see how they worked and then put it back together - sometimes better than it was before. I made upgrades.

As I grew older, I loved to figure out theories and read about what others were doing in the scientific community. I took apart every computer my parents gave me so I could learn how it worked. I also put them back together using different software. I loved computer programming and developing my own software. You might even say that I did things that were not always legal.

Teresa: Were you a child prodigy?

George: I did not think of myself as such, but my parents and other people thought so. I like to think of myself as a regular kid who was inquisitive. I responded well to challenges and loved to compete. I taught myself chess by the age of four.

George laughs. He is a tall, slender young man with jet black hair and the typical untied sneakers, jeans and funky t-shirt that you see every young adult wear. He has longer hair then one would expect given how strict his parents were. He also presents himself as very well rounded and mature. He looks to be around 21 years old.

George: While growing up I had no friends because my parents kept my focus on education. My parents would say friends are jealous. You do not need them. You are too smart for them, and they will make fun of you. You stay home and work on your studies. No time for fun. When you get older you can have fun.

There was no time to have fun, play sports or any other extra-curricular activities that a boy my age should do. Not that sports interested me, but I did not have the opportunity.

My parents were laser focused on me to be a success in the scientific community. They worked hard to be able to put me in private schools, giving me the best education that they could afford. Everything in my life revolved around getting me into the best colleges.

My parents were constantly having me tested and continually challenged me to do better. Nothing was good enough. I had to do better. If I got an A, I was told I should do better, "We want you to get an AA++." We talked about this every day over dinner, and after dinner my father would encourage me to work on my mathematical computer skills.

Then we would talk about it again and again. He would quiz me and yell if I got tired or did not give the exact, correct answer. Our whole lives were about what I was doing. It was work, work, work, all the time.

I listened to my family. That was what I was supposed to do. You follow what your family says. My whole life was waiting to become a success. Each test or competition was a celebration of my success. I looked forward to winning and succeeding at every opportunity.

George: After I graduated college and got a job, there were no more tests or competitions to show how good I was. Nobody was applauding my work. I was just like everybody else at work. I was nothing special.

My boss would often attempt to correct my work or ask me questions, as if I did not know what I was doing. My successes were not acknowledged and people were not in awe of my ideas. I had a hard time at work because there was nothing to look forward to.

My projects at work were not integrated with the other projects, so I did not know how I was doing. I did not know how to make friends at work; this had been one of my many problems my entire life. I did not know how to talk with people.

My father lost interest in me because I could not talk about my classified work, so we had nothing to talk about. I was no one special. I was supposed to be someone special.

One day I walked into my grandparent's bedroom, took out their gun and shot myself.

At this point, I had to stop and take a deep breath...I did not expect this.

Teresa: What made you decide to kill yourself, just like that, one day?

George: I don't know. I just did it.

Teresa: George, you are a very smart man. Why?

George: I do not know.

Michele intercedes and tells me to take a break and that there is another young man, Sam, who has a similar story. He wants to shed some insights on George's life.

I get myself some coffee, and no sooner do I sit down than Sam jumps my perimeter and tells me that he had a similar life but not as harsh.

Sam: George's life was about achievement and rewards. He did not know that there was much more to living. George, like me, was so smart that we had a hard time with social skills. It was easier for me. My parents worked hard at getting me to talk and socialize from a very young age.

I grew up being very intelligent and much smarter than all the kids in class, but not as smart as George. I had loving parents who let me explore whatever I wanted to do.

I, like George, was a geek, who admits that he did not even know he was a geek, because he was so sheltered.

I got to do a lot of things growing up with my parents. They supported anything that I did, whether it was math, science, hiking, planting or painting. I was involved with other activities like karate classes. We took vacations to Disney World, Grand Canyon, Virginia to see Colonial America and many other places. We even went camping and fishing. I had a good childhood. It was school that became the problem.

I was made fun of because I was different, the geek with the big glasses. I was born with a vision issue, and I could not see well, so I needed thick glasses. That, and my intelligence, made me a target. I was harassed by all the kids in my school. I was too smart. I was hurt by all the name-calling, but my salvation was my two good friends who always stood by my side.

We were *The Three Musketeers.* I have known them since I was in kindergarten. They stood by my side all though school. They made school bearable. When I went to college, things changed. We all went to different colleges. I felt so alone and vulnerable. My first weeks at college were difficult. I had no friends, and I did not know how to make friends. When I spoke in a group, I would fumble my words and sound like an illiterate. I felt as if I did not fit in, and even worse, I did not know how to fit in with a new group.

Things progressively got worse. My roommate would often sabotage my stuff. He and many other people on my floor got great pleasure at making fun of me and making me trip or drop things. This was also compounded by the college pressure, new environment and food. Nothing was familiar. Nothing seemed to go well. I felt I did not belong there. I called home and my parents were so positive, telling me just give it time, you will find your way. My parents were usually right, so I decided to try harder.

As the weeks went by things progressively got worse. I started to feel tired and anxious most of the time. I stopped going to the cafeteria for most meals. I had no energy, and all I wanted to do was sleep.

One of the guys on the floor noticed my condition and turned me onto some speed (uppers). That changed my outlook, and I had more energy than I knew what to do with. I was excelling at school again. I was top of my class, and I only needed a few hours of sleep! I was taking these pills every day!

They were great! I felt unstoppable, and it didn't bother me that I was still being harassed. One day when I needed more, the guy I got the pills from got arrested, and then it all came crashing down. I hit rock bottom but so much worse than ever!! I had nowhere to turn. I could not tell my parents. I had no friends. What was I to do? I went to the campus clinic, and they gave me some pamphlets and told me to start counseling for depression.

I went a few times to the counselor, and it didn't help. Meanwhile, my grades were slipping further down a hole. So was I. I took a look around and knew I was in trouble with no way out.

I went home for the weekend and talked with my parents but without revealing to them what I was actually going through. They told me that whatever I wanted to do was fine with them. I could stay home or go back to school. I did not want to disappoint them or have them see me as a failure. I went back, but things only got worse. My experiment in the computer lab failed miserable.

My papers were getting Bs and Cs, even though I had always been a straight-A student. During this time I was doing some serious contemplation and reflection about my life and what was the best I could expect. I knew that committing suicide was wrong. I had read all the pamphlets. I went to counselors, and I tried everything, but nothing was helping. I felt like I was trapped.

I argued with myself for a very long time. I started writing notes to my parents and then I would rip them up and change my mind. Nothing was getting better. My parents kept calling to check in on me and tell me that they loved me. My father arrived unexpectedly one night and took me out to dinner, and we talked all night. He got a hotel room and stayed for a couple of days. I loved my parents, and I was very attached to my father. His staying with me helped.

When I focused back on school, I found myself feeling like I was living my life through a looking glass. There was a thick glass wall between the rest of the world and me; it made me feel numb. I could not take it any longer, so one night after all my letters were written, I decided to take some pills to relax. I relaxed myself right into **HEAVEN.**

114

Teresa: How is **HEAVEN** for you?

Sam: Now that I am here in HEAVEN I can see what I have done to my family, friends and my future life. I know that I hurt many people, and I am sorry for that. I never wanted to hurt my parents. I loved my parents. I was in pain, and it was not going away. I was desperate, and I was not thinking clearly. I regret leaving.

Sam takes George's hand and says to me...

Sam: If George had still been alive when I went to college, he and I would have been friends, and we both would still be living here today. I could've helped George live a life by showing him how to have friends and enjoy life. **WE** would have been each other's support. **WE** would have helped others who were contemplating suicide find the help that they needed. George would have been my mentor in college, and both of us together would have developed a new form of energy that would have possibly changed our energy crisis.

WE would have written a paper outlining how America could avoid being hacked by other countries by using our software protocol. WE would have changed technology in a whole new way. Not to mention we would be best friends and would have raised our kids together. My son would have married George's daughter, and we would have been grandparents together.

It is so heartbreaking for me as I do the interviews, to hear that so many lives were so devastatingly changed and will never be healed, all stemming from one person's decision. If only at that moment when they took their life, they had stopped to think,

"What about tomorrow...?"

What about tomorrow?

I need to rest for a little while, and Michele steps forward.

Michelle: How are you doing?

Teresa: Better. This round of interviews is not so graphic!!!

"TAG TEAM:" We have been doing this for a couple of nights. Let's take a break for now.

It is midafternoon, and I am playing with my kids, when I see this young man sitting at my dining room table. His energy is sweet and gentle. I tell him this is my private down time, and I am playing with my dogs. He responds, "That is why I am here. I love dogs. I like watching you and your dogs. There is so much love and friendship with you and them."

I respond, "Yes, we're all connected."

He tells me that he likes to follow me around when I work with animals and their parents. He stays far in the background, so as not to interfere with my work but has great admiration for my gift to talk to animals. He tells me that when he was here on earth he wanted to work with animals because he felt closer to them than people.

I tell him I understand and that sometimes I feel the same way. He tells me that he and his dog come to my house often. I am uncomfortable with him being here without my permission.

He tells me that my **"TAG TEAM"** let him through so that I would know that he and his friends would be my next interview.

Teresa (to her "TAG TEAM"): Is this so?

"TAG TEAM:" Yes.

With that acknowledgement, everybody leaves, and I continue to play with my dogs.

That night I hear dogs barking, cats meowing and when I look at the clock, it's our usual time, 2:22 a.m.. I had fallen asleep on the sofa again.

I look around the room, and it is filled with **SPIRITS** of both people and animals. I grab my phone, take a sip of seltzer and go to work.

Michele, my "TAG TEAM" and SPIRITS are all bustling around. The room feels unbalanced. I am having a hard time settling down.

Teresa (TO HER "TAG TEAM"): What is going on?

"TAG TEAM:" We wanted you to feel their energy so you would understand their stories.

The young man from this afternoon steps forward with his dog telling me he is happy to be back, and could I let my kids out so he and his dog could play with them as we talk. I let my kids out of their beds, and they crawl up on the sofa with me. All the while the nice looking man with the brown hair and brown eyes patiently waits with his dog for everything to settle down.

My kids are used to **SPIRIT,** and he and his dog have good energy so my kids are calm and relaxed. The young man says his name is Harry, and his dog's name is Brownie.

Harry: Thank you for letting me come and talk to you.

I can feel that Harry's energy is different, like little warm sparks tingling on my skin.

I have felt this before when I have spoken with special needs adolescents who live in HEAVEN. Harry is very comfortable in my house and starts talking faster and faster. The images he sends go by me so quickly, that I feel as if I am on a runaway train. I can't keep up with everything. I can see he is excited to share his life with me.

Teresa: Harry, please slow down, and let's start from the beginning. Let's start with your childhood.

Harry: I had a loving Mom, and she looked after me all the time. She was my champion always making sure that I was ok. My dad, not so much.

He shows me that his dad was more in the background.

Harry: My sister was different than me because she did not have these problems.

She had friends and was able to go to regular classes at school. She went to dance classes, gymnastics, karate and loved music. She had posters all over her room of people she liked and was always on her phone. She was older than me, but she and I were close. But, she was different.

Teresa: How were you different?

Harry: I had problems with the space around me. I was sensitive to light, temperature, sound and certain foods bothered me.

I had many bad experiences in many different situations while I was growing up, mostly due to these sensitivities. I had a hard time doing what other normal kids did, like playing sports, video games or even going to the mall. Even using the computer and phone were difficult for me. The light from the devices was sometimes too much for me to handle. I felt, sometimes, as if I had to live in a bubble to handle life.

When things went bad I would have (what I refer to as) freak-out episodes that would leave both my Mom and me totally depleted. As I grew older, I adjusted a little better, but I still had these freak-out times. I felt so alone.

My mother was my only ally. My sister always defended me. I know she loved me. We did not do a lot together.

Teresa: Did you have friends?

Harry: No. Kids would make fun of me when I first started school. The other kids already had their friends, and since I could not do a lot of the activities, I felt left out.

Teresa: How was school?

Harry: It was not easy. My sensitivities made learning difficult and slowed my progress. I still went to school every day, and I had help from teachers, counselors and aides all through my grade school years.

When I got to high school, I was still in special classes, but I was able to be more on my own without so much assistance. I never felt like I belonged. My mother would always tell me she loved me and that I was important and special, but I never really felt like I fit in anywhere. My dad and I were never close. Most often, he just seemed indifferent. Sometimes I wondered if he was ashamed of me or even loved me. I do not think he understood me.

Teresa: Harry that is a very insightful observation. How did you come to that conclusion?

Harry: I had been in counseling since I was young, and we talked a lot about my dad.

As I grew older, I observed the way he would not interact with me. I shared that with my counselor, and I figured it out. My mom would always be there for me when I needed to talk or when I was swimming or just to sit with me outside on the steps.

My best friend was Brownie. I played with her every day and she even slept with me until I went off to college. I missed her every day that I was gone. She loved me, no matter what. When I had my episodes she would sit right next to me. We would play ball and swim together. During my second year in college, Brownie got sick, and Mom had to put her to sleep. I did not get to hold her for the last time. That whole summer was very difficult for me.

Life at home was never the same without Brownie. I love animals. I wanted to work with animals. My mom even let me volunteer at an animal shelter for a little bit until it got too much for me. I wanted to take every animal home with me. Mom says I got too attached. As the shelter grew, the noise level got too much for me to handle, even while wearing noise deadening headphones.

Brownie is a Chocolate Lab with a sweet disposition, and she shows me that she was very patient and kind with Harry. I can see that she knew he was special, and she took great care of him.

Teresa: How did you go to college with your issues?

He shows me that the college that he chose had programs for people like him, and they would make adjustments for his sensitivities. He would wear special sunglasses and headphones when needed.

Harry: There were others who had worse issues than me. Mom told me that the doctors said I had a mild to very moderate condition. For me if felt very bad. I never understood how they could tell her that it "wasn't that bad."

Teresa: How do you understand the difference?

Harry: My sister was normal. She did not have to have special classes. I did. Everything that I did was difficult. I watched her, and things were easier for her. I saw kids in school, and they did not have to wear headphones or colored glasses. They did not act like me.

Teresa: Did you make any friends at college?

Harry: No. So many of us kept to ourselves, even though there were activities in which we could participate.

Teresa: Is there anything else you would like to tell me about your life?

Harry: I did not like my life. I did not like being different. My mom said I was special. I did not like being special.

All my life I did not fit in. I did not want to be here or there. Many times, I simply did not want to continue. I would think about just not being there. When I went to college, it got worse. I wanted to go to college, but it was hard for me. Everything was different, and I had a hard time adjusting. My mom and sister visited me a lot. I went home as often as I could. I thought a lot about taking my own life. All the time. I talked with my mom and counselor about it. Some days were ok, and some days were not so ok.

Teresa: How did you get here in **HEAVEN?** Please do not show me! Just *tell* me.

Harry: I shot myself.

Teresa: Where did you get the gun?

Harry: My dad had a gun he got from my grandpa. He kept it in the safe. He did not know that I knew where he kept the key. One time when I was home, I got the gun from the safe and took it with me to college.

Teresa: Why?

Harry: It was close to graduation, and I was nervous and scared about graduating. What was going to happen to me? I was DIFFERENT! What was life going to be like with NO school?

At school, I knew each day what was expected of me. I went to classes, and I studied hard. Everything made sense in school. I knew what to expect every day. What if I could not get a job? What if I could not work as a teacher? What would I do each day? What would I do? Everything was uncertain. Nobody had the answers, and I certainly did not have the answers. Each day closer to graduation, it got worse. I felt more scared and angry. I could not sleep, and my stomach hurt all the time. All I could think about was not being there. What if I left? I could not see me having a life after college. One night I went into the bathroom, closed the door, put my headphones on and did it.

I met my grandma and Brownie when I got to **HEAVEN.** I was happy to see Brownie. We have been together all the time since I got here. We go home to visit with mom, my sister and dad. Mom cries a lot and Dad does not live with Mom anymore. My sister is sad.
She has my picture up in her room, and she got a tattoo of me on her back. She misses me. I loved my mother and sister, and I feel their pain. I come to them to let them know that I love them and do not want them to hurt. My favorite sign to them is the smell of lilacs. We

had lilac bushes in the back yard, when I was alive. My mother would often comment that her love for me was as sweet and strong as the lilacs.

Teresa: From everything you have showed me and said, do you like it better in **HEAVEN** than on Earth?

Harry: In **HEAVEN** I am whole. I no longer have these issues. My SPIRIT is healthy. It was my body that could not handle the special light that had been given to me. All those who are here in **SPIRIT** - who were like me when I was on earth - we were special **SPIRITS** incarnated with a unique mission.

We are **INDIGO** Children who are wise and evolved. Most of us are considered on the autistic spectrum from mild to severe. We came to Earth to show men and mankind how to be more sensitive, compassionate and understanding. Our light altered our bodies and caused us to think, behave and operate at a different level. Our intelligence, and the way we learn is unique to us but is the new normal. There are many Indigo Children, both on Earth and here with you tonight, who took their own lives because they could not adjust to Earth. People, regulations and society as a whole have tried to make us conform to what they think is correct and/or normal. We are different.

I now know that and understand that my being **DIFFERENT** was part of a larger picture to help humanity. I did not know that while I was alive on earth. That is why I want my story told to help people understand that we are **DIFFERENT** and we came to be **DIFFERENT**, so that life on Earth can be **DIFFERENT**. We came to change the world.

Each one of us who are called autistic or have mild to severe Autistic Spectrum Disorders including Sensory Perception Disorder, have a unique gift to share with the world.

Harry gives me a hug and smiles.

Harry: I wish I had known that when I was alive on Earth. Had I stayed, I would have become a teacher who would have helped children like me understand themselves. With each generation our evolving understanding of who and what we were, would have helped families, society and the world.

My "TAG TEAM" along with Michelle step forward and says it is time for people to embrace the change and set up new structures for educating society.

It is time to talk about what nobody is talking about......

What Happens The Day After?

CHAPTER NINE
A PICTURE SPEAKS A THOUSAND WORDS

*I*t is a cool day, and I have the window open. I can hear the crows squawking in the trees behind my house. I am drinking a cup of tea waiting for my next reading, contemplating what happens the day after we die. I am lost in my thoughts and emotions, weary from all the stories I'd been told and the images that I have vicariously witnessed. Suddenly, out of nowhere, I feel someone pulling on my shirt. I turn around and it is a young girl about 13-14 years old. She smiles at me and points to my computer.

Teresa: Are you my next reading? Are you here for my next client?

She nods as the incoming Skype call on my computer starts to ring. I answer the call, and the young girl beams with love. I introduce myself to my client and, she, in a thick British accent,tells me her name is June. I ask her if she is from Britain and she tells me, "Yes," and that she is here visiting family and friends, but also lives here in the States.

I ask her how she heard about me, and she tells me that I have given readings to some of her friends in Britain, years earlier. I proceed with my reading, and the first person to come forward is this young girl.

I describe her to June. This girl is about 13-14 years old, blonde hair, blue eyes and is a big girl. I feel as though this girl is June's daughter, so I tell June that her daughter is here and that she is showing me many things. I explain to June that her daughter likes to talk in pictures instead of thoughts or verbal communication, so I ask her to bear with me as interpret what I am being shown.

I also explain that this is not common for loved ones just to simply show pictures.

I proceed to tell June that I interpret this as meaning that pictures were very important to her daughter–she enjoyed taking them, as well as having pictures around her room and her house. That must be one of her hobbies and possibly something she was recognized for. She must have awards. June replied that is exactly how her daughter was. She was kind of shy, had enjoyed taking many pictures and scouting out different places and subjects to photograph. I can see that all at once, June is both relieved and sad that her daughter is here today.

Her daughter is smiling at me and shows me a big heart. I tell June that I am getting a big heart from her. In this case I interpret the heart as her daughter's way of communicating to June that she loves her very much and that she had a big heart when she was here. I am also being shown that she is extremely sensitive and took many things to heart. She had a thin, fragile skin, and what other people said about her affected her greatly.

June remains quiet and I continue to see pictures that this little girl is showing me. I ask the girl her name, and she does not answer. She continues to show me pictures of her doing homework, reading, dancing, being funny and silly in her room and making funny faces at her cat. There are many photos all around the room. She shows me the photo for which she won an award. She is proud of her photography and has many other awards.

She looks happy. I see a report card on the bed and there are all pluses in the margins. She shows me a picture of her talking with June, and the two of them sharing love and that they both enjoyed going to the movies. I relay the information to June.

June: I miss her. I talk to her constantly. How is she doing?

June's daughter gives her a big hug and dances around the room being silly and funny.

I relay that information to June, and then I turn to the little girl and ask her to tell me about her life. The next image I see is the girl talking on her cell phone, crying. She continues to cry and I ask her what is wrong. She turns the phone towards me and shows what I perceive to be text messages and pictures. She then shows me her phone, scrolling and scrolling. I interpret this to mean that there are many pages and possibly many days worth of information.

I tell June that this is what I am being shown. She nods her head and says that, yes, there were many weeks that this went on.

I ask the girl what had happened. She is crying. She puffs her cheeks up and puts her hands outward to make herself look bigger, and I realize that she is showing me that she is being made fun of because of her weight.

She continues to show me many kids with their phones pushing buttons, which I interpret as they are texting her and each other. She shows me social media apps that they are using.

She then shows me what looks like a room with many windows which, I tell June, is a classroom. I feel like the little girl is being made fun of and possibly bullied.

June tells me that this is correct and that it happened on-and-off for months. The little girl continues to show me images of a group of girls that look as if they are the instigators, getting many other kids involved.

Then the little girl shows me that she is back in her bedroom, where she locks the door, and she is crying. She shows me several different outfits that she was wearing.

I feel like this came on rather suddenly. I tell June that she locked herself in her room and did not want to come out for days, including not going to school.

She loved school, but the bullying started quickly and continued no matter how much June tried to intervene.

All of this seems to take place over cell phone technology. I am being shown that very little actually happens face-to-face in school.

I continue, and the girl shows me that they made fun of everything she wore, what she looked like, including her rosy cheeks and her acne. She is very upset and distressed. I ask the little girl again to tell me her name.

She again ignores my request and continues to show me June and her talking with someone else, a woman in an office setting with couches and toys on the floor. There is a small desk with a large pad and colored pencils. The girl shakes her head and puts her finger to her mouth. I tell June that I am being brought into a room that I interpret as a counselor's office and that both she and her mother were there to seek help. But either the girl did not want the help, did not like it or refused to participate. Either way, it did not help the situation.

The little girl tells me that I am correct. They had gone several times to this counselor, and that they made no progress.

Things at school had gotten better, but she felt that the damage had already been done and that no matter how hard she tried, she felt the mean kids were still taunting.

June tells me that she wanted to transfer her to another school but her daughter did not want to go to school at all. It was horrific for them both.

The school initially was not as helpful, nor as proactive as they could have been.

That is one of the reasons why things got progressively worse until June hired a lawyer which helped to the situation get better. But June says that 'Julia'(the first time I learned the little girl's name) was never the same. Her daughter shows me my signs for depression and PTSD (post-traumatic stress disorder). She then takes me back to when she was younger and had a smile on her face, and she was happier. She shows me that she is worried about her Mom and how she is coping.

Julia then shows me many pictures depicting many different situations. As she shows them to me, I watch carefully to make sure I understand what she wants me to know, before telling June. Julia stops.

At this point, I tell June that I can see she is thinking about moving back to England because she feels very alone. Her family and close friends are in England and she misses them. Since Julia's father left, things have been difficult for them both.

Julia worries about Mom and knows that everything that has happened caused her Mom to suffer from her own depression and possibly PTSD (post-traumatic stress disorder).

I tell her that she has not been feeling well and has also developed digestive problems, including intestinal issues like IBS (Irritable Bowel Syndrome). I tell her that she is not sleeping well and has lost several pounds in a short period of time, over four months.

"You put on a good game face for everybody else. You have not told anyone about what is going on inside you. You are not thinking about getting medical help because you keep thinking it will just 'go away.' I am told to tell you to seek medical help. You need medicine and counseling."

June asks me how I can possibly know all of this, and I tell her this is what I was given from Julia. June says to me there is no way I would have known any of this because she has not told anyone about her health issues and has been keeping a poker face in front of everybody. "I have been thinking exactly," June says, "that my health issues will go away on their own." She starts to cry.

June had been trying to stay composed up to this point, and from my experience, the information that comes through can be incredibly overwhelming. I see it as the deer in the headlight syndrome. It stuns my clients for a while, and then it happens: they realize the information is all too real, and that I am talking with their child, and they breakdown and cry.

Julia surrounds June with a big pink **LIGHT** in an attempt to comfort her Mom. At the same time, I can see that June can feel this comfort being given to her. She stops crying and says she feels better.

I tell her that Julia sends her much love and wants to comfort her every time she sees her cry.

June says that sometimes she feels as if she can truly feel her daughter. Julia shows me more images and pictures of her Mom being strong for everyone else, and she had always taken care of everybody else, "including me," but she would never takes care of herself. "She needs to stop worrying about money and legal issues. She still worries about me!!" Julia shows me that she is no longer in pain or anguish. She is happy and right by her Mom's side everyday, sending her messages and signs.

"Mom asks for signs everyday, so I send her the 'red cardinal.' When Mom is in the kitchen looking out over the deck, the cardinal lingers, looking right into the window back at her. I put the TV on while there was one of our favorite movies playing, The Princess Diaries. Then there were weeks with ladybugs showing up everywhere in the house, especially in the bathroom, in her car and at work. All of them were from me. TELL HER, TELL HER!!"

I tell June and her immediate response is, "Yes, Yes. I thought that was her! We would get popcorn and be in our pj's and watch all the Princess Diaries and Shrek movies. Sometimes we would do marathon afternoons…I miss her…"

Julia tells me she also uses the cat as a sign to let her Mom know she's there. The other day the cat jumped up onto her lap while she was crying. She tells me that she also plays with the cat in the house. "That's why sometimes the cat runs through the house really fast. It's because we are playing together."

I asked Julia how she got into HEAVEN, was she ill? Did she have an accident of some sort? She responds with my signs for 'No, No,' and then she shows me a picture of her falling asleep. (I've seen this same sort of thing in the past.)

I now know how she passed.

I asked her, "Did you commit suicide?" She nods her head to the affirmative. I ask her how she did it, and she shows me a bottle of pills. I asked her why, and she shows me that she couldn't go to school. She couldn't go out. She looked in the mirror, and she hated herself. She didn't feel like she wanted to be here anymore. She didn't like the way she looked. Every time she looked in the mirror she saw what everybody else saw, a fat blemished-face little girl.

For the first time in the reading she connects telepathically with me and says"I was so unhappy, and I tried not to show my mother, but I cried all the time. I felt I had nothing. I had no friends."

I tell June that Julia shows me that she took her own life because of everything that went on in school and with her friends. June breaks down and sobs. I ask Julia why she didn't tell anyone, and her response is a blank piece of paper which I interpreted as her not being able cope. I ask her if this is correct, and she nods.

She then shows me these signs: a circle with a line through it, a rope being stretched out tight, and pictures all torn up.

I interpreted this as meaning that nobody knew how hard it was, and that it was happening all the time. Pictures with friends torn up I interpreted, as I had no friends, my life was over.

She then gives me my sign for 'No,' and shakes her head. She then shows me a big heart with a line across, which I relay to her Mom. It means it's not her Mom's fault and that she knows she did everything she could. Julia writes on a piece of paper, I love my Mom. My Mom is my best friend. Mom, I want you to remember the good times. Then I see Julia holding an infinity sign sitting next to June when she is crying.

I tell June everything, including that Julia is with her always. It is not her fault and to stop blaming herself. I keep getting the same image so I keep telling June that it is not her fault.

June looks at me with understanding, but I can see that she still does not comprehend that it is not her fault. She still blames herself. I tell her she needs to get professional help because grief is a very real condition, and she needs to get treatment. She nods.

June tells me that she did not know that Julia was thinking about committing suicide.

She did put Julia in another school thinking that it would be different and had hoped that in time things would have gotten better and this would be behind them.

She says, "I would talk to Julia, and I was under the impression that things in the new school were slowly getting better. I knew it would take time to adjust, and we were going for help."

Julia shows me that it was not getting better.

June tells me that she has been reliving the last weeks before the suicide, "I have been thinking and thinking, "what did I miss?' Were there any signs that I could have missed that would have indicated that she was thinking about suicide?"

I am only able to come up with a few unusual things, but I am having a hard time relating them to her suicide. One thing that I keep rethinking is that Julia did tell me that she was having vivid dreams. In the dreams she was happy, laughing and taking pictures. In most of the dreams she was older and she was in places that were unfamiliar to her.

She told me that she had a dream on another night that she thought was odd because she was with her family. She was much older, her hair was short and there were two young girls calling her "Mom". One of the girls looked just like her and the other looked like the man standing in the background.

We both thought it was very odd because Julia had told me that she did not have vivid dreams or ones that she could remember.

Another odd thing Julia said, was that when she would walk home from school, she would see people that she did not know, smiling and waving at her, as if they were her friends. She did not recognize them, but she felt as if they knew her. I ask if this frightens her, and she tells me that she was not afraid, but that it was, again, very odd, because people in her neighborhood were just not friendly like that. I dismiss it, figuring people knew that she was having a hard time and were going out of their way to be nice.

About a week before she died we got an unknown email from an unknown address with an embedded link containing the words, "Photo Contest."

When we clicked on the link it was an application for a contest to win money for college. Julia said she did not know why we had received that email, because she was no longer taking photos and especially not interested in entering any contest. Everything else was normal.

Julia affirms to me, again, that nobody knew.

I asked June what she thought of these situations. She did not know what to make of them. They seemed to her to be random and not out of the ordinary, but they were still on her mind. I asked her if there were any questions she had for me before we ended our time together.

She asked me to tell Julia that she loves her and misses her.

I asked Julia if she had any final messages. She showed me my sign for love, as well as the cat, and she hugged her Mom, as always. I told June that she loves her and will be with her always. She will continue to inspire the cat as a sign.

I closed my connection and ask if I could comment on Julia's messages. I explained to June that in a reading I am not allowed to include my personal insights nor any additional information I may have gathered during the reading. When I am delivering messages, I deliver them in the purist form possible, authentic to the heavenly client.

I tell her that what I saw was a young girl who was extremely proud of her accomplishments and loved her mother. She was extremely bright and full of promise. Julia did not want to worry you so she kept from you a lot of what was going on.

Unfortunately this situation was more devastating than Julia had let on, and June had no way of knowing. Please forgive yourself and get help.

I explained that the unusual situations that occurred during the weeks prior to Julia's death, were the **ANGELS'** way of interceding to prompt Julia into understanding that there was so much more coming in her life.

They always get involved when a person is contemplating suicide. Their ability to attempt a reality reversal goes to extreme lengths: the unsolicited email, the friendly faces and the dreams.

They will do whatever it takes short of interrupting your free will.

FREE WILL *trumps any and all interference, guidance and support from the **ANGELS**.*

June cried, thanked me for my time and gave me a long hug. She said that all of this information had helped. After she left, Julia came, and I felt a big hug and a loving kiss on my cheek.

CHAPTER TEN
SHINING STAR

*T*oday does not start out like every other day. I wake up very agitated and overwhelmed, and there are moments that I feel as if I cannot breathe. I am anxiety-ridden, my heart is pounding, and I have a headache. I take my blood pressure, and it's through the roof, which is not normal for me. I feel as if I am going to have a heart attack. I consider going to the hospital.

Instead, I decide to take a shower to try to calm things down. I am feeling so overwhelmed that I do not even hear my **"TAG TEAM"** while I am in the shower. The feeling does not dissipate, and it gets progressively worse.

I start feeling as if everything I have done was not good enough and that I need to do things better. I feel like I have post-traumatic stress disorder. I cannot focus, and I do not feel like myself. From my breast cancer, I have some leftover anti-anxiety pills, and I take one. My feelings still do not go away. I cannot seem to focus. All day I feel edgy and anxious like I need out of my life, my head, my home!! I want to scream and cry all at the same time! My skin feels too small for my body, and my thoughts are all over the place! I have thoughts of suicide flash through my mind.

I decide to drive to the hospital that evening, but despite having driven that way many times in the past for my cancer treatment, I cannot find the way. I turn back home, and when I get inside, I take two more pills and fall asleep.

I wake up the next day feeling perfectly fine, as if the previous day had never even happened. I take my blood pressure, it is normal and all my symptoms from the day before were simply gone.

I take a shower and my **"TAG TEAM"** is quiet, which is not unusual. I ask them if I will be fine, and I hear nothing in return, so I continue on with my day until about noon, when it all happens again.

Every negative thing from the day before all comes rushing back. I take a deep breath and stop. I take control of my thoughts and sit calmly on the sofa for a while. This is when I feel as if something is hijacking my energy field. I call on my "TAG TEAM," and they tell me to do a "meditation cleanse." I light some candles and conduct one of my spiritual meditation self-cleansings.

The cleansing helps me feel better, so I decide that I will not cancel my clients today. I am strong enough to work.

My first client is Linda, a beautiful, middle-aged woman. When I opened the door to greet her, I could see that she carried a heavy burden filled with sorrow and anger.

We sit down and I take her hands and open my connection with my **"TAG TEAM."** I am immediately blasted with the very same feelings that have been plaguing me the past two days.

I can not breathe, and the PTSD is so pronounced that I feel as if I am going to faint. I take some deep breaths and ask my **"TAG TEAM"** to *"have him back off of me"* until I can get myself composed.

I now know what has been happening to me! Her son. James, who was passed over, was trying to get my attention to tell me that his mom was coming for a reading!!

James: I was an extremely bright young man in the Military, and I got myself into a bad cycle. I felt bad about myself and my entire life.

Teresa: Slow down, let me get my balance. I will tell your mom everything.

I take another deep breath and close down my connection while I gather my energy. When I am composed, I tell Linda that her son James is here and then I proceed to recount the last two days of what I had gone through.

Linda: That's exactly how James was! He acted like he was Superman. He was always raising the bar, always elevating his expectations, and pushing himself to unattainable levels. All of this made him feel like he never measured up. He did this his entire life. Even when he was a child, I could tell he was exacerbated with himself.

I open up my connection, and James is here.

James: I am with my brother Mark, now. Tell Mom to tell Mark I am sorry. I didn't like the way I treated my brother, and since we are so very similar in the way we think, I now feel that I should have been better to him.

Linda (bursts out crying): I have been asking James to be with Mark. He really needs him now. They had unresolved issues and Mark feels guilty.

Teresa: Have Mark come for a reading so that Mark and James can talk (to James). James, tell me about your life.

James: I was a quiet young man, kind of timid. If I did not know you, I would act like a wall flower. But if I knew you, I was outgoing and funny. I was very smart, but I didn't like to work at school. I did enough just to get by, but no great grades. I loved to draw and had many sketches of animals, people and life. I also was a writer/poet- when I wanted to apply myself. I did get into college, but I lost my scholarship, so I quit.

I had two brothers, but I gave Mark a harder time, wrestling with him and roughing him up. My other brother Tom and I hung out together, but we were different from each other.

James is a very private young man who did not let people know what he was dealing with – his PTSD, his anger, not feeling like he belonged and battles

137

with bouts of depression. As long as he was working and being active, he was able to moderate it, but in his private time and thoughts, he felt constantly anxious and unworthy.

James: I was a very complicated person. My mind would never shut off. I was always thinking and trying to do better – to make everything be better.

Linda: How could James have PTSD? He did not have any situation that would have brought it on.

James (replying immediately): My life felt like it was out of control. I did not know where I was headed, and this was compounded by the way I felt about myself. Add to this the trauma from military life and the precision and intensity in how things were done. This was not me.

On one hand I wanted to go into the military and wanted to learn and find a path for myself, but on the other hand it got to be far too much, far too fast.

I did find my niche though, and I was excellent at what did. I wound up working seven-hour shifts, but this became very difficult for me. For the first time in my life, I had a group of friends that I would hang out with and who I liked.

James: I got involved with them and in their social activities: dinner, partying and late nights, which were tough on me with my work schedule. I started to hang out every night with them and then go straight into work.

I also was conscientious about my uniform and the way I looked. I took a lot of time maintaining my appearance which included ironing my shirts and polishing my shoes. My reputation was extremely important to me. I wound up not having enough time to sleep, and I was becoming very tired. I started taking energy shots to keep my performance up so that I could advance in ranking. I had already advanced faster than anybody else.

Teresa: Is this correct?

Linda: Yes. He was very proud of the work he was doing, and I thought he had found his niche with the military. I am very proud of him!

James: I hang out with my Mom, and I see her writing letters to me. I kept all the letters and cards she sent me while I was away. You know, she found them after I passed. We were very close. I talked to my mom almost every day. Now, I send her signs that I am around. Tell her the red cardinals are from me and that they will always be one of my signs to her, letting her know that I love her and am still with her.

James: I want her to remember the fun times we had together when I would joke with her or tickle her and we would sit and talk together for hours. I remember, as a kid, we would go swimming and I would keep splashing her and when we were in the lake with the inner tubes, laughing and having fun. I loved to laugh and be with my family. See these tattoos – I designed them.

James is extremely proud of these tattoos. One tattoo was a ship with sails and a fish underneath it, with beautifully colored scales. Then I see two birds surrounding the ship.

Linda: He had another tattoo beneath those two with an Indian head. Why isn't he talking about his passing?

James: Please do not remember me the way you last saw me.

I ask James about his passing, and he flip-flops with me as he has done through most of the conversation.

My observation is that he is a very complex, fast thinker with many facets to him. He is so intelligent that he outthinks himself into distraction. In the reading, I feel like I am a ping pong ball trying to adapt to the constant shift in thoughts. I see his actions and thoughts. One minute he is happy, with family and friends, and the next moment he is not, and he strives to be a perfectionist. He is all over the place with his thoughts, from work, personal, friends, expectations and responsibilities.

There is a lot of psychological torture he puts himself through, beating and berating himself for what he has not done or cannot accomplish. The pressure he puts on himself is crushing.

I tell this to Linda and she relays to me that James was a million-miles-an-hour thinker who never shut off. He was a perfectionist. That is why she believes that as much as he loved partying with his new friends, in his last several months, it put more anxiety and pressure on him.

James: I could not bring balance to everything and that started things spiraling out of control. For me it was all or nothing. If I was not going to be the best at something, I was not going to do it. I had no patience or tolerance for the process to unfold. I wanted it immediately.

That is why I only watched my brother play basketball. I would never play with him. I would not even try because I could not be the best. If I did anything I needed a guarantee that I would be the best. I never knew how to just have fun. I never let myself have fun, so when I found friends to party with, it was too difficult for me because I felt awkward and that put more pressure on me to make sure I had fun.

As I explain what James has just told me, Linda recants many stories of her trying to get James involved in activities and him refusing to join.

Linda: I saw him struggle his whole life with himself. He had to be the best at whatever, or he would not attempt it. "

James is listening as his Mother tells me these stories and he laughs

James: I could not deal with failure. I was the only one putting the pressure on myself. There was no one else putting a gun to my head. My Mom tried to help me. She always took the time to talk and spend time with me. She was my biggest cheerleader. She would tell me often that I could do anything I wanted to do, if I would just put my mind to it. I was the one who put the gun to my head.

Teresa: Is that how you died? You shot yourself?

James nods.

Teresa: Before you show me what you did, please stop before the actual act! I do not need to see the completion of your actions.

He then shows me that it was late at night, he was outside sitting on a park bench with tears in his eyes and put the gun to his head.

Teresa (stopping James quickly): Why??

James: I could not do it anymore! I was not able to continue to be perfect.

James: The pressure I put on myself about my job, my reputation and then the humiliation in front of my friends, it was all too much to handle!

Linda: We just found out from the police investigation and friends that the night he killed himself, the girl he was seeing humiliated him in front of his friends and other military personnel at the bar. He was so exhausted, they believe that he was not thinking correctly and that he had never experienced humiliation before and was afraid it would ruin his reputation. So they believe he took his friend's gun, walked out to the quad, sat down and took his life.

James: That is correct. I am so sorry, but I could not see my way clear of this situation. I was a thinker and always had a plan. I had no plan to deal with how people perceived me and what they thought of me.

Linda: How is he doing?

James: I am getting adjusted, but now I spend all of my time with Mom and my brothers. I need to help them right now. Mom is not eating, and you need to tell Mom to start eating. I want to thank her for giving money to a foundation in my name. Tell her I read all the letters she writes to me. It is ok with me for her to take all the letters

141

and put them in a book so that other people can be helped.

Linda: Does James know that I am considering writing a book using these letters?

James: Tell her I sit right next to her and see what she is doing. She needs to stop crying. I feel her pain, and I am sorry that she is in pain because of me.

Linda: Tell him not to worry about me. Is he ok with me talking about him to people, since he was so private?

James: It's ok if it helps other people and Mom. I am all good with you talking about me. I was so shocked at all the people who came to the services. The chapel was filled to capacity. I did not know how much I was loved and respected. I was especially touched by the memorial service on the ship. I had no idea that people thought of me in such a wonderful way. I tried to help others because of my insecurities. I wanted others not to feel the vulnerability I felt. I had no idea that I touched so many people.

Linda: James's Superior Officer had only wonderful stories about him. There were so many wonderful stories that I did not know about how many people he did help. I wish James would have known how respected and loved he was.

James: I did not see myself the way others saw me.

James: I was always trying to prove myself - especially to myself - even at 24 years old, to be respected and viewed as the best.

I can see that he kept himself impeccably groomed and was a handsome, vibrant young man who did not know how loved and valued he was by so many.

Linda: Tell James that I love him and how much I wish he had talked to me before he killed himself.

James: Mom, I love you, and I talk to you every day. Look for the signs that I am there with you. The red cardinal, the dimming of lights and the pennies I leave for you. Did you see the red cardinal today?

Linda replies with tears: When I got to work today there was a business card on my desk with a big red cardinal on it. I asked if anyone had put it on my desk, and nobody know how it got there.

James: I did it. Mom, I LOVE YOU, and I AM SORRY.

Linda, not being able to hold back the emotions, breaks down and cries.

Linda: Tell him I LOVE HIM. He was my SUPERMAN!

My heart breaks for both of them. I give her a hug. She thanks me for the reading, and we talk for a while until I see that she is composed.

I first met Linda at one of my open forums several months prior to our private reading. James was in the back of the room the whole time just watching me deliver messages. He was private, and the message was short and brief.

I had never met her before. I asked her to stand up and say her name. I told her there was a young man in the back of the room, and he tells me that you have a star in your purse that reminds you of him. He tells me he is related to you - he is your son. Linda, shaking, opened up her purse and showed the audience the star she carries in memory of her military son. She said thank you and sat down.

Subsequently, Linda has come for many private readings and open forum events, and James has come to visit, each time delivering specific messages only Linda would recognize.

Both of her sons have been in my office and have spoken with their brother James, and both are still dealing with the accuracy of the messages and the grief of losing their oldest brother.

My forums are open to the public and provide an opportunity for people to experience how **SPIRITS** communicate with the living. I have a very large group of individuals who follow my work and enjoy hearing from their loved ones. I have many clients who have been coming for readings over the last 35 years.

I first met Sophia about twenty years ago when she came for a private reading to talk with her brother. Sophia's reading consisted of many other family members but not her brother. She comes for readings regularly and is at almost every open forum. Over the years, Sophia and I have become very friendly. We have a lot in common. She has become like a sister to me. When we are out socializing or in a reading, her brother has never come through to talk.

Until one open forum, when he stands next to her.

I thought he was there for the person sitting in front of Sophia. Every seat at the event is sold out, so sometimes it is difficult to decipher what **SPIRIT** belongs to which person. Since I never met him or saw pictures of him, I did not know what he looked like until that night. I called on the woman in front of Sophia, and I tell her what he is telling me, but she cannot relate to this information. I see Sophia peer around the woman, looking rather shocked.

Sophia (looking at me): That's Paul.

Teresa: Is this your brother?

Sophia (tearfully and shocked): Yes.

Teresa: He's tall with blue eyes and blonde hair, and he looks very different from you.

Sophia: Yes.

Paul: I am sorry that I have not come to you in the past, I was ashamed. You know I took drugs, and you were told that I overdosed, but I took too many drugs. I knew what I was doing.

Sophia continues to cry and through her tears she asks him why now?

Paul: Because she (meaning me) is writing a book on adolescent suicides, and I have been watching her interview all the **SPIRITS.** I now feel comfortable coming forward to talk to you. I know I will not be judged. **I LOVE YOU,** and thank you for always thinking of me.

Sophia continues to cry

Paul: I am ok. Please don't cry. I love you very much.

Sophia accepts the messages and sits down.

After the event, we're talking and Sophia cannot believe that he came through to speak with her. I can see she is clearly overwhelmed and upset. She has waited a long time for him to talk.

The next day I get a phone call from Sophia, uncontrollably upset and crying.

Sophia: Can I come over? I need to talk.

Sophia arrives at my house in lightening time.

Sophia: I need help understanding what happened last night.

We sit down on my sofa and I explain what happened.

Teresa: Your brother, Paul, was what I consider a 'professional addict.' He had been using drugs since he was 12 years old. Paul sat and spoke with me last night after the event and showed me what his childhood was like. Your father never gave him any attention. Paul played baseball, and your father did not go to any of his games or practices. Paul saw all the other families have their fathers and mothers there, but your family was not present. That really hurt him. Your father did not support nor validate your brother. He did not spend any positive time with him. On the weekends your father was all about drinking, and your mother was all about herself. He felt that all they did was tell him what he was doing wrong. Drugs numbed his pain. Drugs became his way of life. As he grew older and graduated high school, he did not have the support from your parents for college. He had several different manual labor jobs, but was still always using drugs. He felt his life was going nowhere.

Can you relate to what I am telling you?

Sophia: I think so, but I really have to think back. I blocked a lot of my earlier family issues out.

Teresa: Paul had gotten a new job and he needed a physical. He was told he had an enlarged heart and would have to get help. That was all too much for him. He told me he did not want to be on disability. He did not want to be seen as being ill. He did not want to get old and be sick. Do you understand?

Before Sophia could answer, I told her that in speaking with Paul I realized he had never grown up. Even though he was thirty when he died, he stopped emotionally maturing at age 12. When I was talking with him I felt as if I was talking to a teenager with no filters. He had no life skills that would allow him to deal with a health issue. His whole life was about getting the next fix. He did it by being a great worker. He went to work every day on time and did a great job. But he never emotionally matured into an adult that could handle problems, especially one of this magnitude.

Sophia and I sat together for a long while, and I listened to her story and let her feel her emotions. It was an emotionally exhausting day for both of us.

I have been told to include this reading in the book for several reasons.

First, when we pass over into **HEAVEN,** we can take as much time as we need to adjust to eternal life. Living on the other side without a body, is the same as a **SPIRIT** being born into a body.

That is why babies need so much time to sleep and grow. The **SPIRIT** that enters the small body needs to adjust. It is the same adjustment when leaving the physical body, only in reverse.

When a professional addict commits suicide, their emotional scars prevent them from growing up. Paul was emotionally 12 years old his entire adult life.

Not every **SPIRIT** who passes to **HEAVEN** wants to come back and talk. They have **FREE WILL** in **HEAVEN,** just like we have it here on earth. There is no "dial-a-spirit" hotline or phone numbers on the other side. Paul chose not to come back and talk until he was ready.

Respecting the spiritual process is a gift given to all. Communicating with the afterlife is my gift that I chose. I did this in order to share with the world and to help bring healing in both worlds.

Sometimes, it just takes a while for both worlds to connect.

CHAPTER ELEVEN
THE GREATEST GIFT GIVEN

*I*t is a warm spring day, and I am sitting outside on the steps with Wizard and Halo waiting for my next client. I feel a tug on my hair. It is Michelle, and she is happy and excited. She tells me my next client is her mom, and sure enough, rounding the corner is Angela in a bright colorful spring dress, wearing flip-flops and talking on the phone.

Angela hangs up the cell phone and gives me a big hug and a smile.

Angela: How are you doing?

My kids need to get into the action and give her some lovin', as well. We walk up the stairs exchanging weather anecdotes, and Michelle is already talking in my ear. So I get to work immediately.

Angela: I am here to talk with…

Teresa (cutting Angela off): Michelle is already far ahead of you and wants me to tell you that she is so happy that you are back again for a reading.

Angela's eyes start to well up as I tell her that Michelle has been with her and sees her in a new job that she absolutely loves, selling Real Estate. She has only been doing it a year or so, and she is doing very well.

Angela: How do you know that? It's been well over a year since I have been here, and I had another job and career when we last spoke.

Michelle responds: I see everything. I am with you all the time. I watch you sleep, and I watch you work.

Michelle talks about many personal issues that Angela has gone through since our last reading. I tell Angela, and she is amazed how much Michelle knows.

Angela stops me and wants to talk to Michelle directly.

Angela: Michelle, I want you to know that I have sought out help and have gotten individual, as well as group counseling. I have made great progress in coping with your death. I am no longer angry with you, and I want you to know that I feel very bad about the way I originally dealt with your passing.

I was so hurt and angry and wounded and had no room to consider how much pain you had to have been in to commit suicide. I have been trying to put myself in your shoes in order to understand the issues.

I see that Angela's counseling has been a significant contribution to her healing process.

Teresa: Michelle is so happy that you are happy and adjusting to life.

Angela: I had the opportunity to speak with an attempted suicide victim, and that conversation gave me great clarity.

Michelle: I know. I sent my friend from high school to talk to you.

Angela (bursts out laughing): I thought she did!

Michelle: My friend was having great difficulty with some of the same issues that I had, and I knew that talking with you would be healing for both of you.

Angela: It was cathartic for both of us. We both miss you and in our grief we both found that we had a lot in common. We both shared our pain and found out that some of the missing pieces and answers lay within each of our stories. It gave us both an opportunity to see each other's side. We have stayed in touch on a regular basis, and we are both doing much better.

Michelle says that the work that she is doing on the other side is making sure that connections are made. Her work will continue through love so that everything Michelle was supposed to be involved in will still take place.

Angela: Does that mean that she is not in **HEAVEN** or resting in peace?

Teresa: Since Michelle terminated her **LIFE CONTRACT**, she has an obligation to see that it is fulfilled, whether she is alive on Earth or in **HEAVEN**.

Her life -as well as all of our lives – is interwoven with others, including family, friends and society. Since Michelle is not here to help, others will be involved to assist her friend. That is why you gave help to Michelle's friend, because it was in her contract.

Angela: I feel like Michelle's friend has given me more than what I have given.

Michelle: The beauty of **LOVE,** with the intent to heal and help, makes anything possible.

Angela (with a weird look on her face): When did my daughter get to be so philosophical?

Teresa: Michelle has been working with me since our first reading. Michelle has been my spiritual liaison to the suicide community. She has gathered up many suicide spirits, bringing them to my home to talk. I have been inspired by their messages to help others.

Angela (crying): That is just like Michelle, always helping others despite her own need. I miss her. She was my bright shining star!!

Teresa: Michelle is still a beautiful bright shining star! Without Michelle's help, the work we are doing would not have been accomplished.

Angela: How can she do the work to fulfill her contract and work with you?

Teresa: When we become **LIGHT** and live in the **HEAVENS,** we can be in many places at the same time. Like sunlight, when it's shining brightly, everybody feels the warmth no matter where you live.

Would you give me permission to put your readings and Michelle's story in my book?

Angela: You're writing a book about us!!?

Teresa: I am writing a book entitled, Messages from Adolescent Suicides. I have had many interviews with **SPIRITS,** and they want their stories told. I also have in-person readings that I would like to include in the book for readers to understand the communication of **SPIRIT.**

Angela: What does Michelle want?

Teresa: That's why she has been helping me from the beginning. She wants to have her story told to help others.

Angela: Do you think it will help?

Teresa: If the book changes one person's perspective about suicide and ultimately prevents that person from taking his or her own life, then we have changed the world.

Angela: I agree with one stipulation. You have to change everyone's name, and I want to be anonymous.

Teresa: I agree.

Teresa: You should be very proud of your daughter. The work she is doing in **HEAVEN** to help suicide **SPIRITS** is amazing. Her **SPIRIT** has helped many heal including me.

Angela: My daughter was an amazingly bright young woman who is missed every single day!

Angela: Before we end our session, I want to tell Michelle why I came for the reading today. Michelle, I love you, and I will always love you. You are my daughter, my best friend and you are the best thing that I ever did. I will always be your mother, and I forgive you.

CHAPTER TWELVE
LIFE THROUGH A KALEIDOSCOPE

What happens the day after...
High School,
College,
The Big Exam,
The Broken Heart,
The Game Loss,

The Bullying?????!!!!!!!

*W*hen someone takes their own life, that act is the final result of a series of events that have lead this person to feel these things:

- There is absolutely no way out.

- It is hopeless to continue on and believe it will never get any better.

- Most often there have been long term feelings of being displaced. They often feel like they do not belong or fit into family or society.

These emotional experiences are cumulatively compounded with personality and environmental influences. I have come to realize patterns exist that create the profile of the adolescent suicide.

In no way am I saying every reason for suicide is the same, but there are definite traits that these young adults exhibit. The collective accumulation of these traits compounded with family, friends, social and environmental pressures, creates the perfect potential storm for young adolescents to contemplate and then act on their suicidal thoughts.

Scientists have been attempting for years to figure out the pattern of reasons as to why one young adult would commit suicide versus another. There are, however, no clear cut conclusions and no hard answers. I believe we need to address the profile and environmental contributions in order to make changes in the way we raise and support our children.

From my experience, most often these young adults are highly intelligent, whether they are straight A overachievers who are involved with AP courses, or young adults who are so smart they cascade through high school doing the bare minimum, knowing full well that they did not want to put in the effort.

>**1. The A+ student:** These individuals live in a silent pressure cooker. By all outward appearances they are successful and can handle anything. They have the ability to fool almost everyone around them into believing that they are calm and relaxed and have everything under control. This is usually a facade. They are, generally, the academic superstars of their early school years up until and including high school.

>**2. The Quietly Smart Under Achiever:** These individuals do not want to apply themselves. They do the bare minimum to get by, all the while knowing that they do not want to work at anything because it is too hard or difficult. They are either lazy, or they do not want to live up to what is expected from them.

Most parents who have a child like this, and the teachers who have to work with them, know the signs and try to encourage them to engage from within their abilities.

Both categories share extremely alarming statements that I hear over and over every time I talk to a parent of suicide child:

- I never expected it
- My child was the good kid, never gave me any problems
- I never had to worry about them doing their homework or not listening to the rules
- I have other children that give me difficulties, not this child

In the profile, the next most common traits that a lot of adolescents exhibit include the **athlete achiever involved with the extra school activities and/or the artistic performer.** These individuals are so involved in running from one athletic practice to another, or one event to another that they are on the go from morning until night. If they need to do their homework, they do it between classes or on the way to a game, practice or event.

They have very little collective quality family life. They and their family are eating on the run. Between dropping them off and picking them up, family conversations are short and lacking in poignancy. There is, if any, very little time and space for these young adults to experience their family's support and love that has nothing to do with their sports, events or school success.

Most of the focus is on the success of the individual:

Did they win the game?   Were they the best?   Did they score?

This constant focus on success leaves the young adolescent with very little understanding, and very little experience in coping with failure. This, coupled with the constant external focus of participating in group activities, the lack of quality family time, community engagement, and the persistent pressure of just being an adolescent, is why this has become the second most profound trait of teen suicides.

The next personality trait is the lack of true, personal, internal identity and self-awareness.

Most teens feel as if they are not good enough and do not belong.

This begins generating a disconnection to life. This disables them, internally, from forming healthy strong bonds.

Most of them spend their lives defining themselves based on their external influences and factors:

How did I do? Did I win? Was I the best? Did I do my best?

What did my coach/mentor think? Did I live up to their expectations?

Is my family proud of me?

These questions are healthy and should be useful in healthy identity and competition. It is when these questions become the primary focus to this young adolescent's identity, purpose and reason for living that a fragile glass foundation is created. This can be compounded by the stress of always feeling the need to be on top and the drive to get there.

With the goal of winning elevated to the only measure of success, everything else is politely and politically swept under the carpet, further establishing the pattern of inadequate coping skills.

I have found that the majority of adolescents who commit suicide are highly immature. In speaking directly with them, I have discovered the following:

These adolescents have had a demanding, structured life with no time or ability to enjoy any free time.

Parents who do not allow their children to make their own mistakes are creating a foundation of dependency on others to take care of their mistakes for them. These building blocks of dependency generally start when the child is very young in age. Parents who do not allow their child to take the responsibility and accountability for their actions run a high risk of their child lacking the knowledge and the experience to develop mental acuity. Their inability to figure out how to fix or remedy their own mistakes contributes to their lack of self-realization.

First, many parents deflect these issues by rationalizing their child's poor behavior by saying "It is not my child, but someone else's child." This teaches the child to relinquish all responsibility and accountability for his actions.

Second, are parents who all too often take matters into their own hands and step-in to fix the problem for their child. Doing so usurps their child's responsibility and necessary presence in whatever the matter. This results in the child's lack of experience in dealing with failure.

Third, is the parent who refuses to let their child bloom into the individual he or she is going to become. All too often I see parents planning and structuring their child's life without any regard for what the child wants or with any recognition of the innate gifts. The inability for the child to be his or her authentic self generates a sense of displacement and overwhelming feelings of discontent.

Each of the above scenarios represent real factors that contribute to the creation of an immature child who is never given the opportunity to develop the skills necessary to develop life tools. This makes the child unable to be self-reliant and ultimately emotionally underdeveloped in coping with difficult or uncomfortable situations. As the child grows up, each year he or she becomes less invested and more dependent on someone else to handle life for them, which therefore results in disastrous long-term repercussions.

The stigma attached to the words Mental Health is a constant issue. No one wants to be considered mentally inferior or be categorized as being mentally or emotionally ill. In speaking to many adolescent suicides I have found that they are afraid to be labeled as mentally ill. They are afraid that their peers will find out and that they will be judged as incompetent. Their fears are so deeply rooted that they would forgo getting help in order to not be judged. For a young adolescent who is mentally and emotionally developing, this can be a life-threatening issue.

There are many mental health issues that affect young adolescents: bulimia, schizophrenia, even cutting with some. However, the prevailing mental health issue that exists with adolescents is depression, and in the young adult mind, depression is something that 'somebody else has,' or something that 'does not affect me,' hence a wall of denial. Many are afraid that they will be viewed differently, so they feel they can manage the symptoms by drinking, and/or self-medicating.

Some suffer with mental health issues. Many do not even know they have a problem. Worse yet, they refuse to admit they have issues at all, and they think that by ignoring the symptoms, they will go away. Stress, pressure and the demands of high school and/or college life increase the severity of the depression.

Some depression is genetic, and I have found that most families who suffer from a history of emotional issues do not educate their children because they themselves refuse to acknowledge and deal with the problem.

No matter what the underlying factors, depression is a serious and devastating disease that needs attention. It is a reality that most times is very hard to spot, especially in someone trying to hide their symptoms. They almost always project a happy external appearance, and when questioned respond, "Everything is fine."

Every suicide victim has a mental health issue that has never been diagnosed or addressed. Most depression in adolescents develops and manifests over time, with some signs being mild, and others more outwardly noticeable. In some people there are factors that trigger depression, such as a failing grade, rejection or humiliation.

Mental health issues have become a real and growing epidemic that with help and therapy can be managed. In almost all cases, the overwhelming depression in suicide victims wins. These adolescents do not understand the gripping hold that depression has, therefore they do not see it as harmful or life threatening. This, coupled with other factors, alters their reality. The result is the desperate unavoidable thoughts of suicide.

Environmental factors need to be addressed and are a critical ingredient to the young adolescent's view of life. Hand held devices, cell phones, tablets and computers are all major influences in determining the development of a young person's ability to develop healthy life skills. Technology is good if used with discretion and balance.

NO social media and very limited use of computer fun games should be a family standard.

It is the social media and recreational computer games that have created a generations of **20-second-thinkers**. There are apps that only allow you to communicate in 141 or less characters. This form of communication and interactive dialogue is a major contributor in the all out decline in healthy social interaction.

A young adult is being trained to think in such short-term bytes; therefore their ability to think logically through issues is detrimentally impacted. This leads them to process unemotional detached life experiences as if through a looking glass.

One of the life skills that is gravely missing in adolescents is their ability to deal with conflict resolution and problems. They are detached from their actions. They send their ideas and comments into a cloud and it floats away, never to have any effect on them in the here and now. This lack of connection has created generations of what I call the **"No Roots Society."**

Young adults today deal with life on a superficial basis, looking at their hand held devices and engaging only with typewritten words in a social media shorthand, spending hours texting and talking via the comfort of their sheltered bedrooms in their comfortable homes. Their friends are at their cozy homes texting back. Most of the time this interaction is spent in a detached, unemotional, anonymous context where all parties are in a safe, warm environment.

When a person feels safe and secure, they are not vulnerable, and they feel invincible. This leads them to say and text whatever they want with no filters and no boundaries. There are no consequences for their words or actions because the recipient of their texted messages is not in the same room, engaging in face-to-face communication.

Therefore, there is no experience, wisdom and/or knowledge about how the other feels about the text. This void of interaction has led to an absolute emotional disconnect and lack of life skills development.

This type of communication yields a child who has not learned how to engage on an interpersonal level exchanging physical reactions. They also have not learned the art of reading body language and interpreting detailed interpersonal situations. Therefore, when a young adult is out in the world for the first time alone, they find themselves without the skills to engage and interact with confidence. Regrettably, these are strong contributing factors to emotional immaturity.

Another deeply disturbing component of social media is the misrepresentation of life. The exaggeration of how wonderful one's life is, can lead an adolescent, who is already having issues, to adopt a false sense of reality. Many adolescents I spoke with thought that others had a better life than they did. They often describe their life as inadequate and judge themselves based on the posts of others. There is no way to monitor what friends post, but children need to be instructed that not everything they read is accurate.

One of life's lessons we all need to learn, no matter how young or old you may be, is that people only show you what they want you to see.

Most of the suicides I have encountered never matured emotionally because they never had any experiences that caused them to work at growing up. In order to mature into a successful adult, one has to experience personal challenge. Through difficult experiences, personal development creates internal maturity. Nobody can do that for you, you have to do it for yourself.

If one does not see how their words and actions affect another person, how will they ever learn to act and deal with life's situations and grow to a mature outlook on life? That manufactured void in understanding human physical interaction, becomes gravely apparent when attempting to develop deep, interpersonal, meaningful, mature relationships. Most do not even know that they needed to mature in order to feel rooted in their family, friends, relationships and society.

Adding to this already grave issue of child mental and emotional underdevelopment is the ever-growing early use of recreational computer games and the influence they have on establishing quick gratification.

Children, as a direct influence of gaming, have become accustomed to thinking quickly without learning the art of human interaction. Interfacing with other living, breathing human beings requires more thought, feeling and emotion and takes longer than the average 10-second interaction experienced in computer games.

Gaming time is so interactive with the mind that it fails at engaging with the heart and energy of a person.

This has taken away their time to go out and play, learn and experience life with all their senses. The ability to incorporate the judgment required to read a person or situation, utilizing their own internal voice, intuition and fight-or-flight systems, does not develop as it should.

Reasoning skills are also altered by the manipulation of tasks inherent in the computer game:

- Complete a level by doing something and you win a reward.

- Die in the process and you can start the level over with your life restored for a new round.

The child gamer starts to subconsciously view life in the same way as the games they play. In gaming, when you complete a task or a level, you win a prize and are rewarded. If you fail, you start the level over again with a rebooted life. In real life, the drive to continue that gratification of stimulus and response plays out in every aspect of their lives.

This leads to some forms of entitlement:

- **I do not have to work hard for anything; it should be handed to me because I am me**

- **This should not be happening to me, I deserve better**

This type of thought process creates a reality for this young adult that when pressured and forced to rely upon their own skills, crumbles their foundations.

In addition to the issues with Social Media, computers and gaming, college life needs to be considered as an environmental factor contributing to the feeling of not fitting in. When a young adult moves from a warm, cozy, supportive home to a dorm room atmosphere, life becomes a game changer for some.

Dorm living involves sharing your life with everyone around you, and there is very little or no privacy. This can be a very hard adjustment for a young adult, most of whom have a hard time living in a small room, sharing everything from their personal space to their bathroom privileges. They feel overwhelmed, and it is compounded with having to deal with roommates that do not respect their personal space, or with whom they simply do not get along. Even if the roommate situation is rectified, rumors can sometimes spread, causing problems of a completely different nature.

We also have to factor in a change of diet. Most colleges do not make regional cuisine as a staple on their menus. This causes some individuals to feel displaced. **Food is comfort for many people.** Some often experience intestinal issues that go unaddressed due to the change in diet. This creates another pothole in the young adult's life, who may already be unhappy with their living situation, their diet and the pressures of college success. Everything in their life that they once knew to be safe and familiar, has now become unsafe and unfamiliar.

I am not, in any way, saying that if your child has all of these traits or environmental issues they are going to commit suicide.

What I am saying is that we need to start changing the way we raise our children, so that the foundation of how they view themselves and deal with life, is strong and can withstand the external pressures.

We need to find ways to substantively put an end to the rapidly growing adolescent suicide rate around the world. We need to have open dialogue as a community, society and families on how best to address the way we are bringing up future generations. We need to start addressing this problem from a young age.

We as a society need to find a way for our young children to be allowed to get out and play without adult supervision. Children need to play with their peers, and allow themselves to form social bonds. They need experiences that challenge them to think, reason and interact.

During this time in their life they will learn how to engage with others using their body, mind and soul to effectively communicate, think and solve problems. This is the direction that we need to return to in order for our children to formulate a healthy view of themselves, their friends and the world.

Children grow up to be adults, but they need the inner child lessons as the foundation for their adult platform.

Young children need to be allowed to grow up and mature. Parents need to let their young children make mistakes and be responsible for the consequences. When a young child is required to think about what he/she had done and what is needed to rectify the situation, it causes this child to develop long-term life skills and to learn about themselves. Having them accept and deal with the consequences of their own actions at a young age, gives the child the ability to develop an understanding that the things they do affect not only themselves, but other people. Over time this process gives them the ability to confidently communicate their ideas and feelings, thereby learning to understand conflict resolution and the art of reading people and situations.

When a child learns these invaluable lessons, they can develop the ability to reason, cope and have foresight into their lives.

Personal education and instruction needs to be done at home, with loving and supportive encouragement under the supervision of the parents, *NOT BY THE PARENTS.*

If children do not learn to think for themselves they will never learn how to function and thrive as adults.

When I am in readings and am shown this issue, I am told to tell the parent everything that I have already discussed to this point with the addition of one very important factor:

When a young child makes a mistake, it is small and fixable without grave repercussions. When an adolescent, who never learned the lesson, makes a mistake, the consequences can be life altering. Parents often feel as spectators watching their adolescent child ruin their life.

Young adolescents need to stop being identified and exploited by the measure of how well they perform in school or on the field. Acing a test, or being the winner, is not who they truly are. Those things are merely components of how they view themselves, not who they truly are on the inside.

They are so much more than the accumulation of their accomplishments. They are individual, beautiful human beings who possess innate gifts that are specifically unique to them and need to be discovered and explored. These gifts are found inside of oneself. They are gifted by the **CREATOR** and are defining elements of who we are and who we will become.

Intelligence is not to be measured or defined by how well one performs in school, but by the application and development of the gifts they were given, and by seeking out the purpose of this gift in their life. Strength and agility is not only a physical attribute, but it is also an internal force that helps the adolescent deal with life. One's identity is developed externally by all acceptable social, family, school, and religious organizations.

However, a person's true identity comes from within the inner light and has only to be awakened by self-exploration.

Gifts cannot always be measured by how much money one makes, or how well recognized they become within their community. True gifts many times transcend the physical, exhibiting their power on intangible scales. Examples of some priceless positive gifts are compassion, self-worth/value, love, forgiveness, strength, friendship, understanding, acceptance, tolerance, and common sense.

Examples of some negative gifts are anger, stubbornness, laziness, and judgmental attitudes.

All of these gifts were given to you before you were born. No purchase necessary. Unfortunately, many people do not value what they have. They only value what they can acquire.

This is where things need to change. These gifts are the essential elements of who we are, and they need cultivation, time and love to grow and develop, especially in a young adult. From their families they need to know that there is love, encouragement and support. This all develops from the understanding of who they innately are as an individual, not simply because they are the best or the brightest or even the winner.

Family dinners, family time, and family fun need to happen almost every day, not just on the weekends or rare occasions. There needs to be a strong foundation of memories that each young adult can reflect on and use to establish their footing in life. Parents need to talk, not text to their children at the end of the day.

There needs to be more verbal dialogue about how they are feeling and dealing with the pressures of school, activities and social interactions. The undue pressure and expectations that some families put on their children need to stop!!

Every child has a **LIFE CONTRACT** that will be executed, fulfilling their life goals and life path based on who they are. Getting into the right colleges, making the top grades and being the best athlete makes one successful at making money. It does not make one successful at living a fulfilled, enjoyable, healthy life.

Money makes life easier only if the life you are leading is authentic to you.

There is no amount of money that brings inner peace, acceptance, love, happiness, identity, and most importantly, peace of mind, especially when you are not living the life that you love. Awareness is the key that every **LIFE CONTRACT** is codependent on family, friends, society, and the world.

No one person can ever be substituted for another.

Everyone wrote their **LIFE CONTRACT,** and they are uniquely special. The very thing that makes them special is precisely why they are needed. They have something awesome to contribute to the world. Other people need them to fulfill their contract. The very big picture needs to be acknowledged and accepted. Their contribution is mandatory for the success of everybody else's contract, both currently living and future generations.

MENTAL HEALTH

The term, Mental Health, needs to be changed. Another, more accurate way to say this can be *Nonstandard Cerebral Health (NSCH).*

Changing the words will change people's perceptions, consequently opening up a dialogue for help. I have asked every suicide victim if there was a way they felt they could have gotten help had there not been the stigmatizing label of "Mentally Ill" placed on them. Everyone said, "Yes," and that they would have not been so fearful of seeking out the help they needed, if they would not have had to bear wearing the moniker of "Mentally Ill."

A public media campaign needs to be launched to change how kids view these words. We need visible role models to step forward to show that depression is a serious disease and with proper treatment you can live and thrive. The depression stigma needs to change by having more education in school about mental health issues and its signs.

It is not only the teachers and parent's responsibility to identify whether or not a child has the symptoms, it is also their peers who will be the ones who will be the first to see the changes in their friends or associates. Young adolescents are highly aware of their peers and the things with which they are involved. We need to get them more involved in identifying a struggling friend or associate. A buddy system should be in place.

College students see each other every day, and notice behavioral changes in friends and colleagues. We need to give them a wellness checklist so that through their observations and interactions they can assess the situation. If we teach these young adults the signs to look for, then they can be the first responders to notify the proper authorities to take action get this person help.

If we start identifying a young adult who is in crisis earlier, then we can be more effective in getting them the treatment they desperately need.

College is a microcosm contained within a macrocosm with its own set of rules and lifestyle. It is unfamiliar and uncomfortable for many and for that reason there needs to be better awareness for those having a hard time adjusting. There needs to be a better system of checks and balances, especially in the first year of college.

One suggestion is that after a month of school there should be a break (possibly a week) for everybody to go home and reevaluate their living arrangements. This might help many find a better way to cope with their changes in lifestyle and diet.

I also recommend that if your child has many, if not all of these issues, have them take a year or more off from going to college. Give your child the greatest gift you can give them..

LIFE... *without* college.

Let them grow up and learn how to live a healthy life coping with a job, significant other, and living without the identity of school to define them. These skills are invaluable and once they have lived and learned, then they can thrive better in a college environment.

The sad truth is that the social media thrives and makes billions of dollars off of kids under the age of 21. With the perpetual onslaught of new handheld devices, built-in cameras and games, and in-phone editing capabilities are all marketed to high school and college-aged kids. While ignoring the social and emotional implications, it offers fast ways for kids to make money by monetizing their handheld videos and selling any manner of item, all without enduring the arduous process of building a tangible network of real people, and the physical struggle of creating something worthwhile.

Perhaps it is time for a paradigm change.

We need to teach our young adults that there is more to life than electronic interaction, they are much more than a test score, a trophy and a diploma – or even a miniscule avatar on some social media platform.

The difficult situations they will inevitably find themselves in are only temporary. Life will change, and although it might take some time, it will get better.

Life is filled with many obstacles, and with each hurdle cleared comes knowledge, wisdom and experience that is well worth living.

Young adults need to understand that there is a full life ahead of them that includes great experiences, wonderful family, amazing friends, adventurous travel, and passionate **LOVE.** This time in their lives is but a small fraction when compared to the rest of their lives. Being in high school and college in no way represents what your life will be like when you are out in the real world – just ask someone who is approaching their 30-year class reunion! It is so completely different.

What defines them, now, will not be what defines them in life. They get to choose who they want to be and how they want to live.

Some find that frightening, because the rules, regulations and scheduling can give them great comfort. For those individuals who need those comforts, they need to know that the structure that school affords can be replicated in life.

The over achievers need to learn at a younger age that winning should never be equated with success. Most adolescents cannot handle going from being the top in high school where they are in a relatively small to medium size community, to college where they might be at the top but there are many others like them and the community is extra large.

I have a saying that I use when referring to the over achievers in high school:

Most feel like big fish in a small pond, but they are a big fish in an ocean.

They do not know how to adjust in college, therefore it is imperative that they have experiences that lead them to understand and know that *success comes in the ability to deal with failure.*

Life after school is about how we deal with life's difficulties and unexpected surprises. The winners in life are the ones who have the life skills and coping mechanisms to take a disappointment and turn it into a bump in the road, not a road block. Being #1 or top in your group is not real life.

When you are outside of college there is no measuring device that quantifies your goodness, greatness or smartness. This lack of understanding leads to not having the ability to ask for help when needed. They feel that they should be able to handle it on their own, which further solidifies the feeling of being alone and not belonging.

Understanding and coping with failure as an individual - and as a group when they are younger - will help with these feelings.

We need to stop running around being involved with so many activities and teach our children to have time for inner thought development.

We need to teach all these kids that no matter what your belief or culture or religion, all anyone needs to know is that there is a **SPIRITUAL FAMILY ("TAGTEAM")** sending them signs every day.

We are never left alone. We are supported and loved. We need to teach adolescents to talk to their **"TAG TEAM,"** either in their head, out loud, or in a journal.

SPIRIT does not care when, why or how much you talk to them. They are devoted to you and only you. They remain with you 24-7. It is as simple as meeting a new friend and just saying, "Hi." Watch for the results. They show their love in so many ways. Opening up your awareness allows the bond between you and them to grow.

Open up your mind and heart by acknowledging their presence and they will let you know they are there by delivering signs every day. This is key for the young adults to feel connected and supported.

Most common signs are pennies, ladybugs, fragrances or the dimming of lights. Once you are comfortable and relaxed in your connection with your spiritual family, working together you can develop your own personal signs.

Practice gratitude by reciting daily affirmations. Identify and examine the positive qualities and attributes of one's self, and life will nourish the body, mind and soul. Basic affirmations are key to helping the young adult adore and respect their life. Doing this on a daily basis forms bonds and attachments to friends, family and life giving the adolescent an uplifting, comforting, happier mindset.

Simple affirmations are often the best place to start. Here are some helpful examples:

Every morning get up thanking the bed for giving you support and the sheets for comfort. Say to yourself I am grateful for the food that nourishes my body. I am happy the sun is shining giving me energy. I am thankful for the clothes I wear, they give me protection.

Being thankful about everything and being mindful, daily affords personal development and maturity.

We need to start implementing personal education at home. One very practical way to begin doing this, is by incorporating a technique that I have developed...

The "ME MOMENT."

The **ME MOMENT** is a quiet time that you set aside for personal self-reflective observations and relaxation.

It can be done several times a day for long or short intervals. This time needs to be free of all external stimuli, distractions and parental supervision. Providing this time creates balance both in the body, mind and soul. Letting the mind rest opens doorways to the imagination and is the gateway to self-discovery. When we take time to imagine, we can see ourselves in different ways, allowing the psyche to explore the inner workings of one's self.

This special time gives the young adult an opportunity to think about themselves and what they have experienced today. It allows them to absorb and process the events of the day realizing information about themselves, friends, and family.

In time they can learn how to go within themselves to find the strength and courage to handle what life has to offer. This can be used as a time of meditation to connect with their **"TAG TEAM."** Developing that connection with their **"TAG TEAM"** allows them to feel connected to a higher and supportive power. This connection often helps diminish the feelings of loneliness and not belonging.

Incorporate deep breathing techniques. As the child learns how to quiet the mind this will allow more oxygen to flow, rejuvenating the body and mind. As your child advances, yoga and/or tai chi is a valuable tool to help keep your child's inner balance and personal energy strong. It also helps bring clarity and peace of mind, which in turn helps deal with life challenges in a healthier way.

Once a young adult has the ability to think clearly and see life as a whole, they will thrive.

During **ME MOMENTS** it is useful to take notes or keep a journal to maintain perspective. It will also help identify any patterns or cycles in one's life. If there is an unhealthy issue brought to awareness, one can seek the help needed.

The power of **SPIRIT** working through your dreams is an effective and easy way for **SPIRIT** to deliver information. Keeping a dream journal helps organize and document the messages.

Further Prevention

As part of the solution to preventing suicides, we also need to have qualified, specialized therapists administering proper treatment. When therapists administer the correct pharmaceutical cocktails and profound therapy along with the techniques discussed in this chapter, the young adult has a better chance of overcoming the constant unhealthy painful thoughts of suicide.

We as a society need to start making these changes outside of the formal education system. That system is driven in the wrong direction. We need to start the personal education at home and in our communities. We need to cultivate better experiences and generate a strong foundation through the awareness that we need to give future generations a healthier dialogue at a younger age.

In talking with these suicides there were no absolutes. There was no blame. They came in love and earnest devotion to help others.

Their commitment to writing this book has compelled me to continue even when I was shattered and exhausted. The stories were heartbreaking and at times devastating for me to listen to and watch.

Each **SPIRIT** took their time, sharing their stories in the hopes that if even one person reads this book and re-evaluates their actions, then it was all worth the reliving of their personal tragedies.

The **SPIRITS** whose stories were not told are equally important in helping me realize and understand the anatomy of suicide. For those **SPIRITS** whose stories are told in the book, I will forever be grateful. I met so many wonderful **SPIRITS** that this experience has forever changed my life, in more ways than I can adequately express.

I want to be clear that in having identified and addressed these issues, this book by no means stands as the only solution to preventing one from taking their own life. That choice is part of the gift we all are given - **FREE WILL.** What we can do to prevent a bad choice is provide positive, healthier experiences, knowledge and wisdom to help adolescents make a better choice to live and thrive.

These have been my observations that have come to me by doing this work for over 35 years. In that time, I have connected the patterns that I have seen, and they by no means represent the only traits contributing to a decision that brings an adolescent to take their own life. Having identified these traits and environmental factors is a start, progressing in a positive direction to get help to so many in need.

There are many reasons that young adults commit suicide. Some of which are not included in this book. The stories included here were actual recordings of readings and interviews of **SPIRITS** who represented the greater majority of issues that contribute to suicide.

There is a smaller minority who take their life for other reasons, and I want to acknowledge that their reasons are equally important and have, nonetheless, left an impact and void in the world.

I do believe that by bringing to light these issues, we as a society, have an opportunity to help change the course of future generations for the better. One day we may have a healthier society for it.

You can potentially stop a person from taking their own life by giving them reasons to live.

What happens the day after?

CHAPTER THIRTEEN
LETTERS FROM HEAVEN

from your TAG Team

*D*earest Child,

You are an original gift made from **LOVE.** You are a Child of **THE CREATOR.** Embedded in the very fiber of your being is a special treasure box filled with gifts placed there by **THE CREATOR.** The treasure inside this box is so valuable, it is hidden deep within you. Your life is a search for these hidden special gifts, and by following the trail of your experiences, you will be given the clues to the treasure inside the box.

This treasure hunt is a daily journey. Each time you unwrap a gift there is another one waiting to be revealed. There are so many gifts to uncover, that it takes a lifetime to discover their purpose, application and implementation in your life. Once you have unwrapped a gift you will learn how to use it and then share that experience with people in your life.

Life is worth living. The treasure hunt involves everybody; you cannot find the gifts without another person. Each person is uniquely suited to assist you in your discovery. Equally important is that you assist them in their treasure hunt for their gifts. You need to know that you cannot be replaced or substituted in the treasure hunt. It is mapped out perfectly with each person playing his or her important critical part.

*My strength my courage, my
self-identity, my compassion, my
forgiveness, my fearlessness,
my acceptance, my patience.
These are all part of your inner journey
of your self-discovery.*

We all have times in our life when we wonder what it would be like if we were not here. Those fleeting thoughts are there to help us evaluate ourselves, and give us strength and courage to continue forward.

If your thoughts are not fleeting, and you are seriously contemplating not living your gifted life to the fullest, please know that you are **SPECIAL** and you are **NEEDED.** You came here with a plan to live a full life. That plan involves and connects you to everybody around you. All life plans are difficult, but what you do not know is that you are already a success. You were given certain gifts from **THE CREATOR** that are especially designed for you. You are the only person who has this unique combination. Your life path is yours to live, love and even, at times, dislike. There are times in life that you will be unhappy, scared and feel displaced. Living the life that you love is not easy at times; sometimes it is outright horrible. It is work to hunt for treasure; however, these experiences are the building blocks to your own inner journey and they bolster your determination to thrive. Some of these gifts result in your own inner illumination, the awareness that there are outside forces orchestrating synchronicity within your life.

We are your spiritual family **"TAG TEAM,"** and we are here to help. You need to know that what you are going through right now is temporary even though it feels as if this will go on forever and your whole world has collapsed.

You fight with yourself trying to negotiate a better deal for yourself with yourself. You feel like an emotional tornado spinning out of control. Your ability to see things in a positive way has been clouded by fear, anxiety and depression.

You have lost your way.

It is our job as your spiritual family **"TAG TEAM"** to help you find your way. We see that you are struggling and are having difficulties with your life. We see your pain, we feel your despair and depression, we hear your thoughts, and we know everything about you because we have been with you since the beginning.

We are all here for you. We are sending you signs to let you know that we are with you always.

Have you seen the pennies? We are sending you physical signs. Look at the penny it says *IN GOD WE TRUST.*

Have you noticed us in people around you? We have been inspiring people to show up in your life.

Have you seen us in your dreams? We are showing you a better time in your life.

Have you noticed us in your thoughts? We are sending you happy memories and positive thoughts.

Have you felt our presence? We walk right beside you every day.

Have you taken time to notice all the signs we send? The feathers, the butterfly, the bird, the smell of roses, the dimming of the lights, the phone ringing but no one is there.

That is us trying to get your attention to stop.

Stop the way you are thinking and look for the signs from us.

Stop hiding your pain because you are ashamed. Stop thinking you have disappointed your family and friends.

Stop being afraid!!!

Stop thinking negatively and start thinking more positively. Start thinking, "I deserve the help. I need to ask for help. I am special. I have a purpose and I am going to unwrap as many gifts on the treasure hunt as I can and share them with the world."

We create situations and opportunities for you to receive help.

Pick up the phone when the unexpected call comes in from a friend or relative. Take time to talk with the unknown person who gives you unsolicited advice. It is us using others to help you. Accept the help. Let people in and you will see what they see. You will be amazed at the beauty they see in you and how much they care and love you.

If you allow the love ... It will change your life.

Ask for help! We are many **ANGELS** working in concert for your survival. If you feel that you have asked for help from a friend or organization and it has not helped, then try another source.

Your story needs to be told, so share it with someone who will give you the guidance and support. You never know, by sharing your story you might be saving someone else's life. Do not be afraid or ashamed for every person has had difficulties. No one lives a life without scars. Asking for help is a sign of success -- failure to do so is an abdication to the ultimate failure.

There are many opportunities for you to get physical assistance.

We will walk with you every step of the way providing guidance and direction. You are never alone.

It is not required that you believe in our daily presence in your life. It is not required that you support a certain religion or culture. It does not matter to us what you believe.

Our job is dedicated to taking care of you in a loving, protective, and guiding way. We do our job because we love you. You are a special and important person. Be aware that there are plans that require only your participation. Your unique gifts matter, you decided to be born so that you could share *YOU* with your family, friends and the world.

Your future is filled with great opportunities and adventures including love, career, friends and family. There are many unknowns in your future but one thing is absolutely known:

YOU CAME HERE TO HELP MAKE A DIFFERENCE AND FULFILL YOUR DESTINY! LET'S DO IT TOGETHER!

This letter is written with the help and assistance of all the "**TAG TEAMS.**" They want you to know that your own unique **TAG TEAM** took part in writing this letter to you.

With love and dedication to you we want you to **LIVE, LOVE, LAUGH** and most importantly *ENJOY YOUR LIFE!*

We will be a part of it with you forever.

Your "TAG TEAM"

from Dan

I am not a man of many words. If I could do it over, I would choose to come to Heaven when I was supposed to, not by taking my own life far too early.

I WOULD COME ONLY WHEN MY CONTRACT WAS UP AND I WAS NATURALLY GOING TO ARRIVE IN HEAVEN.

Arriving in an unnatural way, as I did, is a horrible way to live in heaven. I see the dif wayference between naturally and unnaturally. It sucks being here unnaturally. It is too hard and too much work. I want to live like those who come naturally, as the life they lead is beautiful. I will not be able to live in beauty. It is like me saying that you can live in heaven in a beautiful house on the beach, sipping cocktails for the rest of your life, or you will have to haul trash for eternity.

Which do you choose?

Let me tell you, choose a natural arrival versus an untimely departure.

Dan

from Michelle

*I*f you think it was easy for me to make the decision to take my life you are correct. It was easier then living in all the pain and watching myself fail. I knew I was a disappointment to everybody. Nothing was going right. My grades were slipping, my teammates were unhappy with me, my coach benched me and most importantly I could not handle the look in my parents eyes when I was going to have to tell them I was a failure. Most days I felt overwhelmed, sad and tired. I was constantly fighting with myself to do better, get my head in the game and find more energy to get through the day. The struggle everyday to live was exhausting. The things I had once enjoyed no longer gave me any pleasure or joy. I found life to be unbearable. That is why I jumped off the building and ended it all. What a relief. I thought to myself I am going to be out of pain and all of it would end. My life did end... and another has begun.

I am going to tell you something... the pain does not end, it is simply different. I am in pain for my parents who are suffering from my actions. I am in pain for everybody who loved me - and I feel their pain, for I did not know that I was loved by so many. I feel the pain for the loss of what will never be my future, my children, my spouse. I will not have a life here in **HEAVEN** filled with peace, harmony, and happiness. I will not know what it is like to rest in comfort, sit with my guardian angel in loving peace. I will not have time to enjoy my grandparents or anybody else who is in **HEAVEN**. I will be too busy.

My job now and for the rest of eternity will be filled with work. I must work at coordinating, orchestrating, designing and fulfilling my contract to meet the obligations of my contract thereby helping others fill theirs. I will forever be a prisoner to the decision I made to eliminate myself and my offspring from humanity. I am accountable for my actions that have changed the direction of the history of the world. This is no mild or small task. It has changed my spirit forever.

I now understand that what I was going through when I was living on earth, was as painful, then, as it was temporary, and that it would have changed over time. My parents loved me and would have helped me no matter what. I had so many people who would have given me assistance if I had let them know how much trouble I was in. I could have gotten better. It would have gotten better.

My circumstances in heaven will never change. I will forever be a servant to my action. There is no changing my condition. There is help, but I will be the one helping everybody else. I will live in Heaven, but I will not get to enjoy it.

I think often of the movie It's a Wonderful Life. Removing myself has negatively affected so many people, and now, I will be responsible for that action forever. Looking at my life now, it was a wonderful life.

If you are thinking of removing yourself from life, DO NOT DO IT!!!! ASK for help, and get the help I wish I had.

Living eternal life as a prisoner to my own actions is forever. There is no replacing me or my progeny. That void remains forever.

If I could do it all over again I would have remained and gotten the help I needed. Fulfilling my contract and living a life would be much better for me and my family, friends and my life. You will not know how unbearable the consequences of taking your own life will be until you get here. I live in a loving heaven, chained to my new destiny of fulfillment for others. That is pain and suffering. I have decided to help others who are here, working with Teresa to write the book to send you messages.

From all of us…
No matter how bad it is for you, find help and do not come here this way, under these circumstances. Living in love without having love is eternal pain.

Michelle

CHAPTER FOURTEEN
LIFE AFTER LIFE

What Happens When We Die?

*T*hroughout the years of my engaging in this work, I have had many conversations with my **"TAG TEAM," GUARDIAN ANGELS, SPIRITS** and **THE CREATOR** on this topic. Dying is a complicated process that takes a lot of work. There is so much that needs to happen when we die, that there are teams of **ANGELS** assisting in our passing.

The first thing that happens is the detaching of the golden cord that keeps us attached to our bodies. Our soul then leaves this body through the top of our head and is embraced by **ANGELS OF RESCUE,** our **"TAG TEAM," GUARDIAN ANGELS** and family members. They lovingly wrap light around us to allow the transition to go smoothly. Each passing is as unique as the individual. No two passings are the same!!

ANGELS OF RESCUE are commonly known as Angels of Death. **ANGELS** do not consider death in the same way as humans perceive death. They view life in two stages.

The first stage is an earthly life, when at birth the golden cord attaches your soul to your body. The golden cord is your spiritual lifeline, performing a similar function as your umbilical cord when you are in the womb.

Both cords have the same function: your umbilical cord keeps you connected to your mother, sustaining your life in the womb, while the golden cord keeps your **SPIRIT** connected to your body, giving you spiritual energy and life while you are here on Earth.

The second stage is your passing into eternal life where your golden cord detaches and allows your soul to transition into spirit and live in the **HEAVENS.**

There is no death; there is only life, just in different dimensions and forms.

Therefore, The **ANGELS OF RESCUE** (their preferred title) help us walk over what is known as the rainbow bridge, (as it is fondly referred to) being the connection between Earth and the afterlife. This is where we all walk to cross over into **THE LIGHT.**

Your family, friends and even your pets will be by your side to comfort and love you as you transition into this new world. **HEAVEN** is a beautiful, loving world that embraces only **LIGHT** and **LOVE.**

What Happens The Day After?

Upon your arrival, everybody will rejoice, and you will be greeted with a celebratory party, for this is your new birthday, being born into **HEAVEN.**

You then proceed to the **HEALING HOSPITAL** where you will spend as much time as you need to heal your **SPIRIT** but only if you have experienced a natural passing.

If you have an unnatural passing, your time in the **HEALING HOSPITAL** is more limited. Suicides do have time to adjust but also have to get to work, for their passing does not allow them to rest in peace. Since they took their own life and broke their **LIFE CONTRACT,** they have to coordinate the fulfillment of their **LIFE CONTRACT** from the **HEAVENS.** This is no easy task. This will take, literally, lifetimes of work and healing.

When a person commits suicide they are still accountable and responsible for their **LIFE CONTRACT.** They will have to work hard to ensure that what was supposed to have happened, still does for everybody whose contract was intermingled with theirs. This will require a team of **TEACHERS, GUIDES** and especially **ANGELS** working with him/her to coordinate the work.

When a person removes themselves from this life by their own hand, there is a void left in the universe that will forever be missed.

There will be no one who will be substituted for that individual, and there will be absolutely no one who will take up their personal mission.

If that person who committed suicide was to do something that would change humanity forever, that person's mission is now voided forever. The history of the world and this planet is now changed for eternity.

Transitioning to the **HEAVENS** can be very difficult and complex, even for someone who has passed naturally. For some, they are afraid to die or do not know what to expect. For others, their passing could have been too quick, and they did not realize they passed, so they may be left asking, *"Why?"*

Some did not want to leave their friends, family, pets or home and can be extremely stubborn. This leads to lost souls. My private work at night is to help them adjust and move into the **LIGHT.**

Most natural passings have a hard time adjusting to being without a body. It takes time to learn how to be back in **HEAVEN** and truly in **SPIRIT. HEAVEN** is a complex world with many ascending levels of consciousness. Each ascending level of **HEAVEN** provides a different living **LIGHT** experience each more beautiful and loving than the preceding level.

Once adjusted to **HEAVEN, SPIRIT** allows them to do whatever they want. If you believe you will play bingo in heaven, that is exactly what you will do. If you believe that you will live in a house, then that is precisely where you will live.

THE CREATOR supports whatever belief structure you have in reference to how you will live in the **HEAVENS.**

The **ANGELS** tailor make **HEAVEN** for each one of us. Their job is to be supportive and make the transition as easy as possible. There is no religion, culture or nationality in **HEAVEN**, only **LOVE.**

HEAVEN in its purist form is happiness, **LOVE** and **LIGHT** wrapped around you like a soft baby's blanket.

Once a natural passing **SPIRIT** has adjusted and moved from the **HEALING HOSPITAL** in their own time and at their own pace, they will do what is called a **LIFE REVIEW.**

The purpose of this is to examine what you have learned and not learned from this incarnation. You will review your life based on what you did and how your interactions and reactions affected other people. You will have to live in their shoes as you do your **LIFE REVIEW.** That is the true hell, for there is no hell in **HEAVEN.**

You will experience everything in your life from an outward and inward perspective in order for you to understand your **LIFE LESSONS.** There is no time factor associated with this. I have seen and communicated with people, who for over hundreds of years are still doing their **LIFE REVIEW.**

Your life here on earth has a direct impact on how you will live out your spiritual **HEAVENLY** life.

Suicides, however, are different. Since those individuals have taken their own lives, their consciousness is wide open and receptive to leaving this world. They want out of the pain and suffering.

What they do not realize is that their emotional turmoil remains with them, accompanying them into the afterlife. They will live in the loving **LIGHT of HEAVEN,** but they will have to work for generations correcting the void their suicide has created.

Their **SPIRIT** will be connected via the lowest level of **HEAVEN** which is closest to the Earth. This allows those **SPIRITS** to conduct their **LIFE CONTRACT** fulfillment with greater ease. Therefore, their spirit heals at a much slower rate, simply because they cannot rest.

Adolescents who take their own lives go through a much more specialized process. Since their lives were cut short by the choice they made, they will have little or no **LIFE REVIEW** until their **LIFE CONTRACTS** are fulfilled, which may take several lifetimes.

The biggest factor that plays out with the review is that they did not complete their future. Since the future would have held new life (their children) and countless interactions with others, they will have to address those ramifications with **THE CREATOR** and be held accountable to an unfulfilled **LIFE CONTRACT.**

Every adolescent **SPIRIT** that committed suicide with whom I spoke, has many regrets for leaving this life too early. They have all expressed remorse for their actions and did not grasp nor understand the full ramifications of what they had done. Not until they arrived in **HEAVEN** did they realize what they had done and what price they would have to pay for their actions.

If they had only known then what they now know, they most certainly would have remained on Earth in their life.

RESOURCES
IF YOU NEED SOMEONE TO HELP

Below is information about those organizations and other resources for those with mental health concerns or who are interested in learning more:

The National Suicide Prevention Lifeline: Trained crisis workers are available 24 hours a day through this crisis intervention hotline. Help is offered in English and Spanish.

Call 1-800-273-TALK (1-800-273-8255)

www.suicidepreventionlifeline.org

American Association of Suicidology: Leads efforts in suicide prevention and intervention through research, education and training, with programs on how to recognize when someone could be at risk, as well as survivor support services.
www.suicidology.org

American Foundation for Suicide Prevention: Conducts research and prevention initiatives designed to reduce loss of life from suicide, also helping people whose lives have been affected by suicide, by offering support and opportunities to contribute to their prevention efforts.
www.afsp.org

Suicide Prevention Resource Center (SPRC): Provides prevention support, training and resources to assist organizations and individuals to develop suicide prevention programs, interventions and policies, and to advance the National Strategy for Suicide Prevention.
www.sprc.org/

Brain & Behavior Research Foundation: Provides information on research focused on alleviating mental illness suffering, understanding the causes of various forms of mental illness and improving treatments of disorders in adults and children.
www.bbrfoundation.org/mental-illness-1

National Institute of Mental Health: Provides general information about mental health, a locator for treatment services in your area and how to sign up for clinical trials.
www.nimh.nih.gov/health/find-help/index.shtml

Substance Abuse and Mental Health Services Administration: Each state runs a mental health agency under the aegis of the Substance Abuse and Mental Health Services Administration. To find mental health programs and treatment facilities in your are
www.samhsa.gov/find-help
Call 1-800-985-5990

National Alliance on Mental Illness: A grassroots organization that provides advocacy for the access to services and support for the mentally ill across the United States. Its more than 1,000 affiliate organizations across America also provide education and training for parents of mentally ill children and adolescents.
www.nami.org

The Child Mind Institute: Private organization that provides research, advocacy, resources and clinical care for children and teens who suffer from psychiatric and learning disorders. The institute's website offers a symptom checker, glossary of mental health terms and mental health guide, and a list identifying 11 simple signs that indicate a child may have a psychiatric disorder.
www.childmind.org/en/tools-and-resources/

The American Academy of Child and Adolescent Psychiatry: The organization's website offers links to resources and treatment options, as well as simple definitions for disorders, symptoms and signs of mental disorders, answers to frequently asked questions, a medication guide for parents, clinical resources and expert videos, and other information. The AACAP also offers Facts for Families , a free comprehensive guide for families dealing with children with mental illness.
www.aacap.org/AACAP/Families_and_Youth/Home.aspx?hkey =4e918a42-7a64-4c60-bf12-9c9ef6e48164

Mental Health America: The organization works to provide advocacy and access to quality behavioral health services for all Americans. It has more than 200 affiliates in 41 states. MHA also provides for the general public comprehensive information about mental illness, and offers links to the public for crisis counseling, treatment options, mental health providers, clinical trials and help to pay for prescription medications, among a number of topics.
www.mentalhealthamerica.net/finding-help

The Compassionate Friends: A national nonprofit with chapters across the country. The organization offers help and support to parents and families who have lost a child.
www.compassionatefriends.org/home.aspx

The COPE Foundation: Connecting Our Paths Eternally is a national nonprofit foundation dedicated to helping parents and families cope with the loss of a child.
www.copefoundation.org/

Together Against Sexual Assault: You are not alone.
www.notalone.gov

Made in the USA
Lexington, KY
29 September 2016